A Family's Journey with
John

DAD'S DYING

Mary Van Hemelen
August 1992

CRC Publications
Grand Rapids, Michigan

Cover photograph: Peter De Ritter

Copyright © 1991 CRC Publications, 2850 Kalamazoo Ave. SE, Grand Rapids, Michigan 49560. All rights reserved.

With the exception of brief excerpts for review purposes, no part of this book my be reproduced in any manner whatsoever without written permission from the publisher. Printed in the United States of America on recycled paper. ♲

Suk, John D., 1956-
   Dad's dying: a family's journey though death / John D. Suk.
     p. cm. —(Issues in Christian living)
   Includes bibliographical references.
   ISBN 1-56212-010-7: $5.75
   1. Death—Religious aspects—Christianity. I. Title. II. Series
BT825.S84 1991
236".1—dc20

ISBN 1-56212-010-7
9 8 7 6 5 4 3 2 1

DEDICATION

In memory of my father, Rev. William Suk (1932-1986).
He knows more of Jesus' victory than I dare dream.

CONTENTS

Introduction 7

One: Facing the Facts 11
Two: Angry with God 25
Three: Let's Make a Deal 39
Four: Too Tired to Smile 51
Five: Through the Valley 65
Six: Victory! 79

Suggested Reading List 89

INTRODUCTION

Tolstoy's short story "The Death of Ivan Ilych" is a disturbing portrayal of how Ivan's family, people living at death's door, refuse to face up to Ivan's impending death—in spite of massive evidence to the contrary. Tolstoy writes,

What tormented Ivan Ilych most was the deception, the lie, which for some reason they all accepted, that he was not dying but was simply ill, and that he only need keep quiet and undergo a treatment and then something very good would result. He, however, knew that, do what they would, nothing would come of it, only more agonizing suffering and death. This deception tortured him—their not wishing to admit what they all knew and what he knew, but wanting to lie to him concerning his terrible condition, and wishing and forcing him to participate in that lie. Those lies—lies enacted over him on the eve of his death and destined to degrade this awful, solemn act to the level of their visitings, their curtains, their sturgeon for dinner—were a terrible agony for Ivan Ilych. And strangely enough, many times when they were going through their antics over him he had been within a hairbreadth of calling out to them: "Stop lying! You know and I know that I am dying. Then at least stop lying about it!" But he never had the spirit to do it.

A similar, horrifying inability to confront death is described by Elie Wiesel in his novel *Twilight*. Wiesel's character, Hayim, describes how the Nazis took him and other Jews to a forest where they were ordered to dig vast pits. After finishing their work, the Jews were shot. By a miracle Hayim fell into the pit before he was hit by a bullet. At nightfall he crawled out and returned home, hoping to warn the community of the terror.

Upon hearing Hayim's story, his father, Aharon, said, "Nobody will believe you. They'll accuse you of spreading panic." And, indeed, after hearing Hayim's story, the community leaders left without saying a word, refusing to believe.

In his landmark study of the Canadian religious scene, *Fragmented Gods*, Reginald Bibby argues that the Christian church—especially in its mainline expressions, too often mirrors this tragic "denial" of death. He writes,

> *A society that emphasizes the importance of the here and now is one that is not likely to encourage individuals to ponder questions such as what happens after we die. The result is that even though Christianity has historically had much to say about the issue of dying and life after death, it is not culturally fashionable to give much attention—perhaps even any attention—to such "pie in the sky by and by" matters. So far as culture dictates religion's emphasis, it is only to be expected that concern with the afterlife would not be given a high priority by some, and perhaps most, of the country's [religious] groups . . . . If religion does have something to say about dying, death, and hope, then the time has come for [religious] groups to quit echoing culture's non-message. If they have something to say on the topic, they need to speak.*
>
> —Fragmented Gods: the Poverty and Potential of Religion in Canada; Toronto: Irwin, 1987; pp. 248-251.

This study booklet is written to take up Bibby's challenge. From my own pastoral experience with dying people, I've concluded that Bibby is correct: even Christians have a difficult time pondering death and eternal life. The church needs to speak to the issue. Refusing to face up to death, as described by Tolstoy, Wiesel, and Bibby, will eventually rob us of the hope implicit in Jesus' resurrection, the good news that "Death has been swallowed up in victory." As the apostle Paul says, "'Where, O death, is your victory? Where, O death, is your sting?' . . . Thanks be to God! He gives us the victory through our Lord Jesus Christ" (1 Cor. 15:54-57).

At Redeemer Christian Reformed Church in Sarnia, Ontario, many members took the time and effort to encourage and instruct me as I ministered to dying persons and their families. This booklet is one of the fruits of their support and encouragement. I'd also like to thank both Redeemer Church and the Ann Arbor Christian Reformed Church for making the writing of this booklet possible through their provision of generous time away from regular pastoral duties for study leave. Finally, thanks to Irene, Billy, and David, whose desire to know how it came out in the end was a constant encouragement for me to get there myself.

—John D. Suk

ONE

FACING THE FACTS

April 19, 1987
Dear Diary:
    Today, for about the tenth time in my life, I'm going to start a diary. Dad gave it to me for my birthday.
    Writing in a diary has never lasted long with me before—mostly because my life has been so boring. Grade 9, though, at least so far, has been a different story! I love school. Mostly I love David. He looks so cute in his hockey uniform! I only wish David would look at me.
    Before I get too far into these deep things, I should introduce myself. My name is Janet Smit. I live near London, Ontario. I have a mom and a dad. They both work at the Petrosar plant here in town. Mom does computer stuff, and Dad sells rubber. I have two brothers: Peter is in grade 13, and he's crazy about computers, just like Mom. John is done with college, married to Sally, and teaching. They've got two little kids, Ralph and Scott. I go to Happy Valley Christian High (not kidding), and my best friend, Deb, is at Myrtle Beach for the holidays. It's freezing rain here, and I can hardly stand it.

April 4, 1988
Dear Diary:
    When Dad got back from the hospital today, he told us he was all done with his physical therapy. He said it was five years ago this

week that he had had the car accident! I was only in grade 5 then (1983), but I remember it like it was yesterday. I remember going to the hospital and seeing him stuck with all those tubes and wires and cables. I asked Mom if Dad was dead, and I'll never forget how she said "I hope not!" and how scared I was when I heard how she said it. Later I learned that both of his legs were broken, he was bleeding badly inside, and he had a fractured skull. He couldn't talk for weeks. The minister had been there, and he had prayed with all of us. I'd never cried in the middle of a prayer before. That was five years ago, five years of operations, therapy, rehab, and so on. And now it's finally over!

March 26, 1989
Dear Diary:
   After church David asked me if I wanted to go see My American Cousin with him on Friday night. As if he had to ask! Hope Mom will let me stay out just a bit longer for once.
   I have to do my presentation on AIDS for health class tomorrow. I can't believe the things they say about that disease. If what I've read is true, millions of people are going to die of it—and not only homosexuals. I know it was wrong, but in my heart of hearts I didn't really worry much about AIDS when I thought it was only for homosexuals.
   I asked Mr. Hull, our religion teacher, what the Bible says about AIDS. He said that one Bible word, the Greek word eplagxnisthey, could really help us understand how to respond to AIDS. You get "all tied up in knots inside" when you try to say the word, Mr. Hull said, and that's just what it means and just what compassion is supposed to feel like. We should get all tied up in knots inside for people with AIDS—no matter who they are. (I still think that would be hard for me to do if the person were a homosexual.)

December 3, 1989
Dear Diary:
   I'm worried about Dad. He looks horrible. He's lost weight, I think, except around his middle. And his skin looks yellow, like some jaundiced baby's skin. He can't swallow, and I hear him getting up at night—I don't know how many times. He coughs a lot too. Mom thinks maybe it's our new house, an allergy to the formaldehyde in the walls or something. Dad is sick of doctors, but he'd better go see one soon.

December 31, 1989
Dear Diary:
   The party's off for tonight. They say Dad has AIDS.

◆ ◆ ◆

Mr. Ralph Smit was resting, not very comfortably, in his doctor's steel and glass waiting room. He was running a hand up and down his arm, looking at the floor. His wife, Diane, was sitting close by, pretending to look through an old *National Geographic*. When the nurse called Ralph's name, both Ralph and Diane stood up. He put his hand on his wife's back, directing her gently toward the door the nurse had opened for them.

Diane found herself wondering how many times the two of them had been here since Ralph's accident. First it had been the seemingly endless series of examinations for his left leg, which had never set right. After that he had developed an ulcer, and, lately, jaundice. But this time it was different. It was as if they had never been here before.

Diane's tone before they'd entered the office had been tired and defeated: "Ralph, the doctor must be wrong. You can't have AIDS. It's ridiculous—you're barely fifty!" He had wanted to pray with her then, but even after thirty years of intimacy, real prayer was still their last unconquered abyss. Now Dr. Cross was waiting for them in her office with the same old desk and diplomas and dusty silk plants. A bad sign. Didn't she know better than that? It was the same place she had told him his leg would have to be reset.

"How are you, Mr. Smit? Mrs. Smit? Please sit down." Cross sat behind her desk. Ralph saw that it gave her space. Safety. Distance from him. As she spoke the words, Ralph realized how dumb they were. But they would have to do, because there were no good words. "Well," began the doctor, clearing her throat, "I have the written test results. Ah, there's no mistake. I'm sorry to have to say so, but there's no way around it, Ralph. It really is Acquired Immune Deficiency Syndrome."

"What about a second opinion?" asked Diane.

"It's your choice, of course. I have the name of a doctor who has worked quite a bit with AIDS in our community. But we all have to use the same lab. It's the only one."

"No. Yes. I mean, we'll go to one of our friend's doctors. We might not need an AIDS doctor."

"Well, it's your privilege. I can't tell you what to do, but I'm afraid a second opinion won't change things. I know it isn't easy, but you'll have to face it, and the sooner you can do that, the better. It really is AIDS. From the transfusions."

Diane again. "The lab could have gotten the test results mixed up with someone else's. That's happened before, hasn't it, Doctor?"

"Sure, Mrs. Smit. But I don't think . . ."

"So a second opinion only makes sense. And AIDS, from what I know, is a tricky disease. It's hard to detect."

"Yes, but . . ."

"Well, we'll just have to be very careful, that's all. Personally, I think the problems have to do with Ralph's gall bladder or something like that. The kids still need a father, after all . . ."

Diane knew better, thought Ralph. In times of crisis—like when he had his accident—she was the towering strength, the family crutch. He looked at the door. He wanted to go home.

"There is something else I need to talk to you about, Mr. and Mrs. Smit—something that has to be looked at. You see, Mrs. Smit, it's important that you get blood tests too."

"Why, Dr. Cross? It hasn't even been established that Ralph has AIDS. Why should I be tested? Nothing personal, Dr. Cross, but it seems as if you have jumped to conclusions here."

While his wife grasped at straws, Ralph wrung his hands. The doctor had said *she* needed tests. It wasn't possible, was it? All day long he had been thinking hard thoughts: How much insurance did he have? Was AIDS covered? Would Diane bother cooking every day when he was gone? Should she and Janet move closer to John and Sally? Would Diane get married again? What would she do with the new cottage on Lake Huron? What does a coffin cost? Heaven . . . Hell . . . His father, nearly eighty, in a nursing home. Hard thoughts.

What had the doctor said? "Mrs. Smit, it's important that you get blood tests too." Ralph had thought the same, but only in the deepest corner of his mind. He hadn't had the courage to let those thoughts register. Till now.

The rest of the visit passed quickly. Muttering protests, Diane rolled up her sleeve. Rubber band. Clenched fist. Cotton. Alcohol. Needle. Closed eyes. Tube. Another tube. Red. More swabbing. Bandage. Stand up. Doors. Drive. No one speaking. Home.

When they drove in the driveway, everybody was waiting. Ralph's eyes were filled with tears. At the open door, he and Diane were held, embraced—even though the weather was rushing in cold behind them. Laughter. Diane making noises like all would be okay—as soon as they found another doctor. Diane describing her tests, explaining that the results would be in tomorrow. And during it all, Janet didn't say a word.

So, thought Ralph, this is dying.

◆ ◆ ◆

Rev. Venema had not yet heard from Ralph and Diane Smit, but he had already heard the news. One of the things that surprised him no end was the efficiency of the church grapevine. He wondered if he should go straight over to the Smits' but decided against it. He would give them a day to get in touch with him first. But then what? Not four weeks in the harness, and already he had this to deal with. The oldest seminary joke went through his head:

> New pastor calls up old professor: "Sir, I need help. Someone in my church has just died!"
>
> Professor: "Don't worry, son. We covered that in ministry class. Find your notes and read them over."
>
> New pastor: "But sir, that won't help. This guy is really dead!"

The joke didn't seem so funny anymore—only true. And his situation was even worse: his dead man was still alive.

Still, why not just see what his notes said? In fact, didn't he write a little paper on death for theological reflection once? After a bit of rummaging around, he found it.

Defining Death, by Lewis Venema

> Rev. Eppinga once related a conversation he overheard between two members of his congregation. They were at the funeral of a mutual friend who had been suddenly killed in an accident. "That's how I want to go. Quick," said the first friend.
>
> "Not me," said the second friend. "I want to die in bed. I want to gather my children around me for a last talk about their eternal welfare." Eppinga wrote that in due time he buried both of them. Neither got his wish. The first friend, the one who wanted to die quickly, died in bed—slowly. The second friend also died in bed. But he never gathered his children round for a talk about their eternal welfare. By then he didn't know them anymore.
>
> Before anything else is said, one should be clear about the fact that death is perverse and horrible. From Genesis to Revelation, the Bible teaches us that death is a curse that follows in the wake of our sin.
>
> But what is death, exactly? It isn't as simple a question as you might think. Webster's Dictionary defines death, in part, as the "permanent cessation of life in a person, animal, or plant, in which all vital functions cease permanently." According to the dictionary, then, death occurs only when all the following things happen: when the heart stops pumping blood and the brain stops transmitting waves and the liver

stops manufacturing chemicals. This "biological" definition of death has some problems, though.

The trouble with this definition is that modern medical technology has made it possible to keep at least some of a dying person's vital functions going almost indefinitely. As I write this, Victor Davis, a Canadian gold-medalist swimmer, is in a deep coma in a Montreal hospital after being struck by a car. His prospects for recovery are poor. This morning the news announcer said, "In case of his death, Davis's body will be kept alive to save his vital organs so that they can be used for transplant." How does one keep a dead person alive? Do ventilators, infusion pumps, bladder tubes, and dialysis machines just extend life—or are they a substitute? A Dr. Rosenthal wrote in Discover magazine that when ICU doctors were asked how their shifts in the Intensive Care Unit were going, they were apt to say they had been "watering the vegetables."

The very trouble we have in defining the moment of death, especially where modern technology is involved, suggests to me that death is something more (or worse) than a terminal condition of our flesh and blood. Death can't be described as a moment in time. Actually, death is an ever-present, dehumanizing power outside of ourselves. At least the apostle Paul thought so. He wrote, "Our struggle is not against flesh and blood, but against the rulers, against the authorities, against the powers of this dark world and against the spiritual forces of evil in the heavenly realms" (Eph. 6.12). Romans 8:38 makes it plain that Paul believed death was one of those dark powers. There Paul writes, "Neither death nor life, neither angels nor demons . . . will be able to separate us from the love of God that is in Christ Jesus our Lord." Or again, in 1 Corinthians 15:24-26, Paul writes of the last days: "The end will come, when [Jesus] hands over the kingdom to God the Father after he has destroyed all dominion, authority and power. For he must reign until he has put all his enemies under his feet. The last enemy to be destroyed is death."

It helps me to think of it this way: Shakespeare once said, "All the world's a stage," and he was right. According to the New Testament, our world is a stage on which the cosmic drama of creation, fall, and redemption is being played out. We are actors in that cosmic drama, but so are the powers that Paul writes of. Death plays the role of Satan's femme fatale. *Mostly, Satan simply directs her to wait in the stage wings, ever patient, always ready, to pounce upon any of us who come within her reach—as we all must, eventually. Then she becomes intimate with us and our friends and family. She bloodies and disfigures our young in accidents; she makes the elderly forget and lose control. Death leaves children without parents, fashioning great big holes in the lives of the living, holes that are hard to fill. Death is a power that works tragic drama in our lives.*

As a power outside of ourselves, rather than simply a final moment we must all endure, death is usually at work in our lives long before we actually experience physical decline. We humans, after all, are more than purely "physical" creatures. We are embodied souls. Some theologian says we are a "psychosomatic" unity, from the two Greek words that mean soul (psycho) and body (soma). We need both a body and a soul to be fully human. As a power outside of ourselves, death need not go to work on just our bodies; it can also work in our souls. While we are alive, death will always do its "damnedest" to separate our souls from God.

The fear of death's power, for example, was what drove Adam and Eve to try to hide from God after they sinned. The redemptive good news, of course, already in Genesis, is that God does not surrender us over to the power of death without a battle. Rather than abandon Adam and Eve to the power of eternal death, God clothed them with the divine assurance that they would be redeemed from the grave.

Again, as a power outside of ourselves, death tries to pry us loose from God. According to the writer of Hebrews, death does this by enslaving us to fear (2:15). Elsewhere in the New Testament, Paul says that before becoming alive in Christ, the Ephesians "were dead in [their] transgressions and sins in which [they] used to live when [they] followed the ways of this world and the ruler of the kingdom of the air, the spirit who is now at work in those who are disobedient" (Eph. 2:1-2). Redemption, on the other hand, means becoming "alive with Christ" (2:5), being close to Jesus.

With that, Rev. Venema put the paper away. It had more to say, and, judging by the grade it received, it said it well. But Mr. Smit—and possibly his wife—really had AIDS. Venema felt helpless and preoccupied. Even prayer didn't seem to help. He had to preach again tonight, and it was New Year's Eve. It was time to get ready, and in light of the news about Mr. and Mrs. Smit, he had never been quite so nervous about a message as he was about the one on Psalm 49 that he had written for this evening. It went like this:

> Dear Friends of Jesus:
>
> Nobody wants to die. A Mutt and Jeff cartoon from long ago puts it this way.
>
> > Said Jeff to Mutt: "I wish I knew where I was going to die."
> >
> > "Why?" asked Mutt.
> >
> > "Because," said Jeff, "then I would never go there."
>
> We laugh at Jeff's nonsense, and yet it strikes close to home. The truth of the matter is that the world is full of people who are trying with all their might not to go to the place where they will die; if they go there by mistake, they refuse to admit as much. It's called denial, but it doesn't work. The writer of Psalm 49 knows that. He says, "No man can redeem the life of another or give to God a ransom for him—the ransom for a life is costly, no payment is ever enough—that he should live on forever and not see decay" [vv. 7-9]. The writer of Psalm 49 means you can't buy death off; you can't deny death and get away with it—at least not forever.
>
> Still, our world is full of people who are trying with all their might not to go to the place where they will die. Let me offer a few examples of how people try, foolishly, to deny death's reality for themselves. While I do so, ask yourself, "Am I like that?"
>
> At least half of all Canadians try to deny the reality of their own deaths by refusing to go to a lawyer to make sure their wills are in order. Others, even some here this evening perhaps, refuse to come to grips with their declining health by refusing to make arrangements for where they will live when they can no longer live at home. To speak of chronic care or nursing homes strikes too close at the frailty and brevity of their lives.
>
> The psalmist mentions rich people in particular as being prey to thinking they can somehow deny death's reality with their riches. They trust in their wealth and boast in their riches. Is it possible that some of us refuse to think of death by concentrating on paying off our mortgages or by buying more than enough RRSPs or by saving to buy a trailer in

Florida? The psalmist says fools die too—people like Susan, of whom C.S. Lewis wrote,

> "She's interested in nothing nowadays except nylons and lipstick and invitations. She always was a jolly sight too keen on being grown-up."
>
> ". . . Indeed . . . . she wasted all her school time wanting to be the age she is now, and she'll waste all the rest of her life trying to stay that age. Her whole idea is to race on to the silliest time of one's life as quick as she can and then stop there as long as she can."
>
> —The Last Battle; Macmillan, 1956; p. 135.

This world is full of Susans, full of people ill prepared to consider death and prepare for it; the world is full of fools of every kind who live denying death. But the Lord says, "All can see that wise men die; the foolish and the senseless alike perish and leave their wealth to others" [Ps. 49:10].

Do you live denying the power of death? I know a parable you ought to consider, then.

Once upon a time, a young man found a stranger badly bruised and hurting in a ditch. He tenderly bathed the stranger's wounds and gave him a drink from his canteen.

"Do you not recognize me?" said the stranger to the young man.

"No," said the young man.

"I am Death," said the stranger. "I spare no one. However, in order to show my gratitude to you, I will not call your name until I have sent my messengers to give you a fair warning."

The young man was pleased that he would live safe from the fear of death. He continued to live a happy and carefree life. But youth and health did not last long. As the years passed, illness and pain tormented him by day and gave him little rest by night. But the man always said to himself, "I may be sick, but I will not now soon die. Death has not yet sent his messengers." Still, one illness followed another. His days were uncomfortable, and the road to recovery was very long.

Finally, though, his health was restored, and the man began to live joyfully again. "I will live a long time," the man thought. "Death still has not sent his messengers." Shortly after his health had returned, the man heard someone calling his name. Turning, he saw Death standing beside him. "Follow me! Your hour of departure from this world has come," said Death.

"What!" cried the man. "You are going to break your word? You promised to send your messengers before you arrived. No one has warned me."

"I am surprised you did not recognize my servants," Death replied. "I sent Fever to slow you down. Next, Arthritis came attacking your joints. Later Gout gave you aches and pains all over your body. Finally, I sent Sleep to remind you each night that death was near." The man had no answer. He yielded to Death that very hour and found that he had finished traveling to the place where he would die.

>—"The Messengers of Death," a German folktale; reprinted from Stories for the Telling by William White, copyright © 1986, Augsburg Publishing House. Used by permission of Augsburg Fortress.

This evening, the last evening in the old year, is one of God's messengers of death. Please be wise to it. Time passes. One year flows into another. Our lives will come to an end.

Are you ready to die? Do you know that you must die? Or are you like the fool in Psalm 49—one of those people who will not, cannot awake to death's power in their lives? If so, remember what the psalmist said, "No man can redeem the life of another or give to God a ransom for him—the ransom for a life is costly, no payment is ever enough—that he should live on forever and not see decay."

New Year's Eve is a God-given time for all of us to think about our mortality. I do not intend to be a spoilsport before you go to parties and family gatherings. Go, and enjoy yourselves, because God means for us, in Christ, to rejoice always. But go as wise women and men, as women and men who know about the horrible crisis of death that sin has thrust upon the world. As you leave church tonight, go as people who understand the preciousness of the gospel, of the psalmist's confession that in the face of death, only "God will redeem my life from the grave; he will surely take me to himself" (Ps. 49:15).

Suggestions for Group Session

Opening

Read the parable of the rich fool from Luke 12:13-21 or the following version of Psalm 49 in contemporary language:

> *How foolish are the creatures of God!*
> *They accumulate wealth*
>   *and imagine themselves secure*
>   *in possessions and property.*
> *Or they utilize some inborn gift*
>   *and dote on the plaudits of their peers.*
> *They live for themselves alone*
>   *and give no thought to eternity.*
> *They claim that God is simply*
>   *not necessary to their existence.*
> *He is just a big thumb in the sky*
>   *designed to pacify the weak and childish.*
> *They claim that man must be*
>   *sufficient unto himself.*
> *He doesn't need the extra baggage*
>   *of faith or religion.*
>
> *But when the riches melt away,*
>   *health fails, talents wear thin,*
>   *and remaining talents become few,*
>   *when no one honors them*
>   *or expresses concern for them,*
>   *then they stand naked and exposed*
>   *in empty despair.*
> *Their fortress is breached;*
>   *they are flattened and defeated.*
> *Life, what little of it there is left,*
>   *no longer has meaning for them.*
> *Then they may look desperately for the God*
>   *whom they discarded in their youth.*
>
> *Let us consider carefully the security*
>   *of a loving relationship to God.*
> *Let us mouth His praises*
>   *and demonstrate in our lives the eternal joy*
>   *of knowing and relating to Him.*
> *We need not depend on this world's wealth*
>   *nor the accolades of men.*

> We need not fear the end of our days
> upon this earth.
> God is forever—
> and so the souls of those
> who are committed to Him.
> Clap your hands, shout for joy!
> God is real, and He is here!
> —From Psalms/Now by Leslie F. Brandt, © 1973
> Concordia Publishing House. Used by permission of CPH.

For Discussion

1. In *On Death and Dying*, Elisabeth Kübler-Ross writes, "Denial functions as a buffer after unexpected shocking news, allows the patient to collect himself and, with time, mobilize other, less radical defenses" (p. 39). She adds, "Denial is usually a temporary defense and will soon be replaced by partial acceptance" (p. 40). Kübler-Ross also notes that nearly all of her terminally ill patients eventually do accept that their illness is terminal. Jesus addressed his own disciples' continual denial of his prophecies about his death with patience and gentle persuasion. See Mark 8:31-33 and 9:30-32 as well as John 13:36-14:4.

   In light of all this, how would you evaluate Mr. and Mrs. Smit's denial—hers of her husband's illness, and his of the fact that his wife might have AIDS too?

2. How do the "raising from the dead" miracles remind us of the fact that death is a principality and power (1 Cor. 15:24-26)? For examples, see Mark 5:35-43 (Luke 8:49-56), Luke 7:11-17, and John 11:32-44. Similarly, how does Jesus' own death remind us that death is a power outside of ourselves? (See especially the accounts of Jesus in the garden of Gethsemane.) Ought we be comfortable with the prospect of dying?

3. Elisabeth Kübler-Ross also suggests that the belief in life after death and the belief that suffering on earth is rewarded in heaven are both ways in which Christians "deny" the reality of death. How would you respond?

   (Here I like the punch line of "The Parable of the Severe Winter" [found in *The Music of God* by Segundo Galilea; Oak Park, Ill.: Meyer Stone Books, 1988; pp. 24-25]. In the parable a pastor is chastised for preaching of a coming day of warmth and plenty, because it distracts people from doing what is necessary to get through the harsh winter. The pastor replies, "Not to speak of summer would indeed be a disservice, for then the people would not be considering their reality as a whole, with the hope that is part of it. Moreover, you can see for yourselves that just because the people are waiting for summer does not mean that they stop trying to overcome the problems of winter and make it more bearable and human.")

4. Here is a list of personal matters related to death that need our attention. Cross out the items that do not apply to you (your parents may have already died, for example). Then, from the remaining list, circle the items you have not yet attended to. Share your list with the discussion group, telling them (1) how you feel about your list and (2) what you are going to do about the items that apply to you.

   a. I/we have a will that is up to date.
   b. The will includes provisions for the dispersal of family heirlooms and keepsakes.
   c. The division of my/our estate as outlined in my/our will acknowledges in a very real way that my/our material blessings are a trust from God to me/us that God intends I/we use to help make his kingdom come.
   d. I/we have chosen and notified guardians for my/our children in case of death. The matter is attested to in the will.
   e. I/we have enough insurance to provide for survivors in case of my/our death.
   f. I/we have discussed death and what it is all about with the people I/we love most, including any children old enough to understand.
   g. I/we have discussed the following with my/our parents, siblings, or children in the case that I/we become elderly:
   1) future housing needs
   2) preferences about funeral arrangements
   3) whether to use life-support measures if there is no reasonable expectation of recovery from physical or mental disability.
   h. I/we have continued to visit the surviving spouse of a deceased friend as often as I/we did before the friend died.

5. Mr. and Mrs. Lake are in their mid-eighties. They have managed quite successfully to live on their own as they have grown elderly. However, because of a stroke two years ago, Mr. Lake has been unable to walk farther than a few feet at a time without tiring. He enters the hospital frequently with various minor complaints, all of them real, but none of them serious enough to

keep him there for long. Mrs. Lake is very healthy, but caring for her husband is beginning to tire her out. She no longer has time or energy for friends or other family members. The Lakes have a son and daughter-in-law who are both nearing retirement age. They are faithful children, doing whatever they can to enable the elderly parents to stay in their home. The Lakes' other, younger children live hundreds of miles away.

The son and his wife would like to retire early and spend half of each year in Arizona, especially since Mrs. Lake, Jr., suffers from arthritis and asthma. They speak to the Lakes, Sr., about moving to a combination retirement/nursing home. The Lakes, Sr., will not hear of it and become extremely angry at their children, charging that they have selfish motives for wanting their parents to move to a retirement home. The Lakes, Sr., quote passages such as Exodus 20:12, Ephesians 6:1-3, and especially 1 Timothy 5:1-8 to their children. The Lakes, Jr., go to their pastor for advice. What might he say?

Closing

Pray for openness and candor as you discuss your attitudes toward and feelings about death. Then close by singing a song of triumph over death's defeat by Christ's resurrection: "The Strife Is O'er, the Battle Done" (*Psalter Hymnal* 391; *Rejoice in the Lord* 319).

TWO

ANGRY WITH GOD

March 26, 1990
Dear Diary:
    I just came back from the hospital. Dad is much the same. He's started with AZT now, and antibiotics for his lungs. The doctor won't promise that Dad can come home soon, though. I had an awful thought when I walked into his room today. The bed he's lying on is probably his deathbed, his last bed ever.
    I hate that hospital room. People you've never seen in your house in ten years suddenly start acting like it's the patient's dying wish to spend time with them. I always end up sitting on Dad's bed because Mr. Important Elder needs my chair, or I get sent out of the room because the Women's Guild is dropping by for a mass revival. All of this to a never-ending chorus of "Nurse, nurse" from a man with Alzheimer's who is otherwise perfectly healthy.
    Come to think of it, the only place I hate worse than the hospital is church. I don't want to go there. They sing songs like "When Peace Like a River." What I'd like to know is "where?" I don't see any peace.
    Do I still believe? Sure. But believing with anything like a bit of enthusiasm takes more out of me than I've got. Religion-wise, I'm kind of like watery soup stock—there's potential, but not much else. Dad gave me a book by C.S. Lewis, A Grief Observed. In it, Lewis describes his reactions when his wife died: "It's not that I am (I think) in much danger of ceasing to believe in God. The real danger

is of coming to believe such dreadful things about him" (pp. 9-10). True. So I don't want to go to church. Why, God? Why do you have to drag us through the muck and kick us all over?

March 28, 1990
Dear Diary:
　　David. (I can't believe I ever liked him. He's all jock and no brain. He's going to be a great carwash jockey some day.) He came up to me the other day and asked if there was any way I could get AIDS from my dad. What he really wanted to know was if he could have gotten AIDS from me (from kissing!). I wish he'd drop dead. Moron.
　　Mom. How come she doesn't have AIDS? Logically, she should. She's married to Dad, after all. But she gets off, while Dad gets hit by a one-in-a-million bad blood transfusion. God has tricks up his sleeve. Lewis calls God a cosmic sadist for making him suffer. If I had read that a year ago, I would have slammed the book shut. Not anymore.

April 1, 1990
Dear Diary:
　　At the hospital Dad treated us like we're a bunch of demons sent to torment him. He complained on and on. Why didn't Mom bring up the Globe and Mail like she promised? He started muttering about how it was always the same with Mom, how she always promised and usually forgot. When Mom handed him the book Megatrends (why he wants to read it I'll never know), he said he supposed now that Mom had remembered one thing, she probably expected thanks—as if she were doing something above and beyond the call of duty. What a bear.
　　Big brother Peter finally went home last night. I'm afraid he didn't have such a good visit either. He and Dad got into a fight about creation and science. Peter has really gotten into it in a big way ever since he took that teaching job in Watford. Dad thinks he's crazy, and he's been buggin big bro with all this stuff about why can't he be Reformed instead of Fundi—as if it matters when you've got one foot in a hospital bed and the other in the grave. But Dad kept it up for three days straight, and by the time Peter left the hospital yesterday, he was crying. When I asked him if he was okay, he told me to get off his case.
　　Seems like it isn't enough that Dad's got AIDS. Seems like we've got to put up with a lot of other stuff from him too—and most of it's nasty.

❖ ❖ ❖

Mr. Smit's disease, AIDS, earned him a private hospital room. Officially, it was provided so that Ralph could get the rest and quiet he would need to fight back some of the opportunistic infections that eventually make AIDS fatal; unofficially, Ralph got the room because in a small town like Happy Valley it was easier to isolate him than it was to explain to roommates that AIDS wasn't catching.

Ralph's room was the hospital's most decorated. At first, his church family had been confused and frightened by the AIDS diagnosis. Later, though, after one of the council members, a nurse, gave a short lecture on AIDS after the morning service, the members of Ralph's church had responded in the only way they knew how in such circumstances: they swallowed hard and, in spite of disgust and fear they hardly dared admit, sent cards and candy and chrysanthemums. Many (probably too many) came in person. Most of them massaged his back, watched TV with him, played chess, and read him books. But some of Ralph Smit's visitors came with other things on their minds.

Mr. Friedrich Konig dropped by one Saturday afternoon. He was Ralph's credit union manager. He sat down in the twenty-year-old steel and plastic easy chair opposite Ralph and smiled.

"Hi, Ralph."

"Fred." Fred was not Ralph's favorite person. Too much a debits-and-credits sort. If you bought a car, Fred was sure to entertain you with a tale about how he could have gotten a better deal for you at the dealership down the road. If you wore a new suit to church, Fred wanted to know what you paid for it. Fred always wondered why he had never been promoted to vice-president of his firm, but these kinds of indiscretions demonstrated to all who knew him exactly what his problem was.

"How are you?" Fred was trying. The question might well be an old saw, but still, it was the best.

"Lousy." Ralph was in no mood to humor Fred or to take solace or comfort in Fred's attempts to reach out and touch him. Nothing was good. The food was lousy, his family wasn't sitting by his bed day and night, and he had let the life-insurance policy lapse last fall. Ralph knew, of course, like most good Calvinists, that he was totally depraved, that he had no right to expect or bank on grace, and all that. On the other hand, long experience had taught him to appreciate the good things in life, the cozy things. "Life is rotten and unfair. I know it sounds stupid, but that's how I feel. I feel like someone—God, I suppose—has kicked me in the mouth, and I'd like to kick back."

"But, Ralph, you shouldn't say things like that about God." Fred was on the edge of his chair. "God must have some good reason for all of this. If you think about it, it should come through eventually."

"God's good reason, Fred, must be that he wants me to die. And I'm not ready."

"But there must be a good reason for God wanting you to die. The ledgers have to balance between you and God somehow. There must be some accounting going on, Ralph."

"What do you mean?" Ralph lifted his tired bones off his mattress and leaned back on his elbows to get a better view of Fred. "What do you mean? Not that I deserve this, I hope!"

"But in some way don't we all deserve what happens to us? Doesn't God say something like . . . wait a minute, I have to look in the Bible, it's somewhere in Jeremiah . . . ." Fred, like many members of his church, knew the Bible in general pretty well, if not by verse and chapter. "Here it is, in Jeremiah, chapter 17, verse 10: 'I the LORD search the heart and examine the mind, to reward a man according to his conduct, according to what his deeds deserve.' And that's in line, don't you think, with all those covenant passages in Deuteronomy that talk about blessings and rewards?"

"Get off it, Fred. You make it sound like I'm sick because I'm bad. Don't you remember what Jesus said about the man born blind—that neither he nor his parents had sinned?"

"Sure, but that's for people born with diseases. You came down with this later in life. Like in Corinthians, when unworthy people were going to the Lord's table, they experienced divine discipline so that some were sick and weak and others died. And doesn't Paul say in Romans that God gives people over to their sins? Couldn't your AIDS be because of your sin, Ralph? Maybe a sin that you're not aware of? Maybe something you ought to confess but haven't? Confession is good for the soul, you know."

Ralph hissed then, and loudly for a man in bed with severe respiratory problems. He spit the words out, spacing them evenly, like sawteeth. "Get out . . . . Leave . . . . Move it, Fred. Take your stupid sins-and-blessings ledger with you too. Out!" And Fred left.

Later that afternoon, Sister St. John from the hospital's pastoral care department dropped by for a visit, as she often did. She was pushing a small cart. "I have your supper here, and mine too. Can we sit and eat and talk for a while?"

"Sure."

Sister St. John arranged the crank-up table, raised the crank-up bed, and turned off the television. Then she pulled back the stainless-steel covers and ripped off the plastic wrap on both of their meals. Ralph's food was mostly mash and puddings, because the huge sores in his mouth made it hard for him to chew. Finally, both settled, Sister St. John started. "The nurses say you made life pretty miserable for them yesterday. You had them in six times in one shift to fluff your pillow or move your bed. Your wife left in tears. She wouldn't talk to me—you people tend to stick together when it comes to taking care of each other—but it was pretty obvious to everyone at the desk that you were raising your voice at her. Dare I ask you how you're feeling?"

"Look, sister. I don't want a fight. I've got enough on my plate without another fight."

"I suppose you have a right to be angry. What can I do to make you feel better? I saw Mr. Konig leave. He's upset patients before."

"You would be upset too, if you were dying and someone came in and suggested that it was all your own fault—even if he didn't actually say it."

"Right . . ."

"And if it isn't my fault—if I'm no better or worse a sinner than the next person in the pew, then why am I here and not that next person? Can you answer me that?"

"I don't know why you're in the hospital, and I agree, Ralph, that you are no more or less deserving of this tragedy than anyone else. Why do you think this happened to you?"

Ralph knew the rough-and-ready answers he had been taught since childhood. He had heard them rehearsed many times from the pulpit. And he sensed that Sister St. John was fishing, pushing him to get some more control of himself than he had had of late. But didn't he deserve to be angry? He was dying.

"Well?"

"I suppose the minister would say I am sick because of sin—not my personal sin necessarily, but the power of sin let loose in the world."

"You mean just because everyone else sins, you pay the piper?" asked Sister St. John.

"Well, yes and no. One of the ways of experiencing sin is as a kind of pollution. That's the analogy our pastor uses. Imagine a chemical spill in the St. Claire River. If I were to swim in the river, that pollution would surround me. It would hurt me and anyone else who was swimming there—even though we didn't know about the pollution and even though, strictly speaking, the pollution wasn't our fault. All of us who swam in that water would be at greater risk for cancer, but only some of us might get it. There's just no telling. Just so, people come down with diseases like mine. They're caused by the pollution of sin in the world, and there's no telling who exactly is going to come down with them. Some kids get leukemia; most don't. Some babies mysteriously die in their cribs; most don't. Sin, like pollution, is an impersonal, malevolent, ugly power that invades and pervades our lives. No one is totally immune from it, but no one is guaranteed to come down with AIDS or cancer or a stroke on account of it either."

"Does that mean that when bad things happen to average people, it's never their fault?" asked Sister St. John.

"Of course not. Sin can be personal too. Sometimes bad things happen to people because they have been bad. Many people who have AIDS lived sexually promiscuous lives or used drugs. Bank robbers get shot at and killed by the police. People who commit adultery watch their home lives go to pot."

"Or," continued the nun, "sometimes bad things happen to people because others have been bad to them. A chaste and innocent wife might get AIDS from a husband who is having a homosexual affair. Bank robbers kill innocent bystanders."

"Right. But am I supposed to feel better now? So what if I can say I have AIDS because of the pollution of sin in the world—why did God ever allow sin at all, then? It's a hackneyed question, I know, but suddenly, from the comfort of my deathbed, it seems pretty important to me."

There was a knock on the closed door. Janet entered. "Hi, Dad. How are you feeling? I brought you a milk shake."

Much to his surprise, Ralph heard himself say, "Better, Janet. Come on in. Have you ever met Sister St. John? We've been having a deep talk."

"Hi." said Janet. Reaching over the bed, she gave her dad a big kiss and hug. Then Janet sat down and held her dad's hand. "What you are talking about?"

"About why good people like me get AIDS, especially if God is good."

Janet looked in surprise at her dad. Then, head down, Janet said in a whisper, "To be honest, I've been wondering the same thing myself. I'm having trouble today believing God is very nice. I'm angry. Everybody is angry." Janet raised her head and looked belligerently at Sister St. John. "I'm angry at God, and it makes me feel bad, but not bad enough to give it up."

"God can take it," said Sister St. John. "God even expects it. You've stumbled on something the Psalms are full of. Think of Psalm 22, for example: 'My God, my God, why have you forsaken me? Why are you so far from saving me, so far from the words of my groaning?'"

Mr. Smit spoke up, slowly. "Pastor Venema was here. He read Psalm 88. It ends like this: 'You [God] have taken my companions and loved ones from me; the darkness is my closest friend.' It made me sick to hear it, at first. But Rev. Venema explained that this psalm was in the Bible, in part, to let us know that it's okay to complain to God. We don't have to feel guilty about it."

"So it's not a sin to be angry with God—at least not for a while?" asked Janet. There was some genuine interest in her voice. "But that still doesn't help me understand why God is doing this to us. Why? What do the theologians say? Do they have any good answers, Sister St. John?"

"I'm not sure that what the theologians say from their ivory towers is always very helpful when the patient is down in the pits. But do you really want to know?"

"Maybe," said Janet. "It's either that, or I go on being angry at God."

"Well, I'll try to sketch out a few of the main answers. One important thing to keep in mind is that whatever else we say, we want to hang on to the God of the Bible. Our answers to the question of 'Why do we suffer?' have to allow for God being both good and all powerful. We can't very well say, 'We suffer because God isn't powerful enough to crunch sin,' or, 'We suffer because God doesn't care much for us, because in his eyes we're less than ants.' Are you still with me?"

Janet nodded her head. "I think so. However we answer the question 'Why?' we have to make sure our answer agrees with the Bible, which says God is good and all powerful."

"Right. The most common way of doing that, and the one that I feel as if I can make some sense of, has it that we suffer because of the ruin we as humans brought into creation by our sin. And we sinned because God created us with choices, with freedom: we could choose for God or against God. If God had not given us that freedom to choose, we would have been less than human. We would have been like robots or computers, which can do only what they're programmed to do. The trouble with freedom is that we might choose wrongly, against God. And that's what happened, of course."

Janet looked confused. It was a long answer. She nodded hesitantly. Her father had fallen asleep. He did a lot of that lately: in the middle of conversations or when watching the Maple Leafs with friends, sometimes even between moves of a chess game. Another irony. Only a few months left, at best, and he had to spend them sleeping.

It was raining outside, and in the dim light of dusk even Sister St. John was beginning to feel down. She decided to take one more stab at it. "Janet, the bottom line is that we don't have very many good answers and maybe no satisfying ones. Why is your dad dying instead of one of the prostitutes down the street at Ruby Tuesdays? I don't know. As God says in Isaiah 55: 'My thoughts are not your thoughts, neither are your ways my ways . . . . as the heavens are higher than the earth, so are my ways higher than your ways and my thoughts higher than your thoughts.'

"God's thoughts and ways are over our heads like some of the farthest stars are over our heads. We can't see those stars with even the most powerful telescope. You see, just as it takes time for me to drive from here to my mom's home in Toronto, it takes time for light to travel from one place to another, from star to earth. But some stars are so far away from the earth that even though their light shines, that light just hasn't arrived here yet. So even though those stars are there—beautiful, awesome, and shining—we can't see them or know very much about them. They are too far above us. Just so, God's thoughts and actions are above us. We can't see their purpose or their symmetry, even though both are surely there."

Janet thought about what Sister St. John was saying. "But not understanding doesn't help me, Sister. I'm still angry." Her voice cracked, and tears streamed down her face. She whispered, fiercely, "I wish God would just roll up his sleeves and get to work in my life and in Dad's, sweep them clean of some of the garbage that fills them up."

"I heard a true story the other day," said Sister St. John. "It's almost too terrible to tell—but still it fits. There was a boy of twelve or thirteen who, in a fit of anger and depression, got hold of a gun and shot his father. Then the son stood there, watching for a while, till it was all over. When the police asked him why he had done it, he said that it was because his father was always demanding too much of him, because his father didn't give him everything he wanted. He did it because he was disappointed in his father."

"I know how he felt. I'm disappointed in my Father too," said Janet.

"Well, the boy was placed in a house of detention. One night, soon after, a guard was walking down the corridor late at night when he heard sounds from the boy's room. The guard stopped to listen. The words that he heard the boy sobbing out in the dark were 'Daddy, Daddy, I want my daddy.' That's us."

Janet sat quietly for a while. She was disappointed in God, all right. Disappointed enough to shoot him, she figured. And, still, she couldn't let go.

Sister St. John got up to go. As she passed by, she took Janet's hands in her own and gathered her up in a hug. "Keep coming to see your dad, Janet, even if it hurts," Sister St. John whispered. "And if he's angry, let him be angry. Just keep on caring for him. Even if you have nothing to say, don't leave your father alone. Feed him. Kiss him. Touch him. Laugh in his presence, and cry with him if that's what he's going to do. Being here like that won't answer any questions, but it will help you to endure, to be like Jesus for each other." With that, she left.

◆ ◆ ◆

Pastor Lewis Venema had just returned from visiting Ralph, and as was often the case, the visit had left him with many questions— especially the question of theodicy. Why did God let people suffer? Why the way of the cross? Lew sat in his office chair with a cup of coffee, thinking about it. If God could have snapped divine fingers so that death didn't rule our planet, Lew would not have argued. If a magician God could pull eternal life out of a sleeve like many-colored hankies, there would be no objections from Pastor Venema. But Lew knew that death was a troublesome enough enemy for God, and that defeating it had involved God in a costly struggle.

Yet what an odd struggle. Jesus never descended upon Judah with legions of angels, and he wouldn't descend upon North America or Russia with bomber fleets of seraphim. The dark powers made things happen by forcing events, by exerting pressure, by making threats, and by pointing guns. But even under Jesus' command, battalions of angels armed with M-16's could never coerce people into loving God or being good.

Jesus had to reject coercive power. Paul says in 1 Corinthians 1 that just as the weakness of God is stronger than human strength, God chose the weak things of the world to shame the strong.

So instead of beating back evil with force, God did it with the cross. In some mysterious way, God in Jesus won a victory over sin and evil by suffering with and for us, even to the point of death, and then emerging on the other side—not unscathed perhaps, judging by the scars, but resurrected and glorious. At the same time, Jesus, in suffering for us, in becoming weak for us, demonstrated the lengths to which he was willing to go on account of his love for us.

It occurred to Pastor Venema that what suffering people really need are people who are willing to suffer along with them, people willing to share the load. It's not that theodicy isn't important—it just doesn't make the pain go away. Jesus didn't come to explain God's ways to us; he came to share our pain with us and so to relieve us of some of the burden of it.

Lew thought about that, both his hands round the warm coffee cup. Jesus really suffered. After Luke 3, we never hear again about his father Joseph: Rev. Venema imagined Jesus at Joseph's grave, holding mother Mary's hand. Early in Jesus' life, his cousin John was executed for preaching the same gospel that Jesus had begun preaching. Just a few months later, Jesus cried at the grave of his best friend, Lazarus.

Jesus suffered. Mark says his family rejected him as a madman. His Nazareth neighbors responded to his preaching by trying to lynch him. Jesus ended his life abandoned and alone, in the hands of foreign soldiers who whipped him and spat on him, nailed him to a cross, and left him. Jesus, left innocent and alone in the dark, cried out, "My God, my God, why have you left me?"

Jesus suffered. If we say God is good, we ought to say it on account of God in Jesus loving us to the death. If we say God is powerful, it must be with the knowledge that although Christ rose victoriously from the grave, it was still an awful battle and a dark struggle for him to break the bonds of death.

Lew shuddered. Death could never be God's fault; if it were, God would never have paid such a steep price to ransom us from it. There is no explaining God's ways. But we can know where God's way leads. It lands God at our bedsides and in the midst of our tears. God's way is to take over enough of our suffering so that it doesn't overwhelm us. God's way leads to Ralph's bedside so that Ralph need never be alone.

Lew picked up the book he had been reading, *Lament for a Son* by Nicholas Wolterstorff. "It is said of God," Wolterstorff wrote, "that no one can behold his face and live. I always thought this meant that no one could see his splendor and live. A friend said perhaps it meant that no one could see his sorrow and live. Or perhaps his sorrow is splendor" (p. 81).

Suggestions for Group Session

Opening

Read Psalm 88, the psalm Pastor Venema claimed teaches us it's all right to complain to God, and Isaiah 55:6-9. Then offer sentence prayers to God, each asking for strength and healing for someone you know—someone who is ill and possibly dying.

For Discussion

1. Reflecting on the death of his son, Nicholas Wolterstorff asks,

   How is faith to endure, O God, when you allow all this scraping and tearing on us? You have allowed rivers of blood to flow, mountains of suffering to pile up, sobs to become humanity's song—all without lifting a finger that we could see. You have allowed bonds of love beyond number to be

painfully snapped. If you have not abandoned us, explain yourself.

—Lament for a Son, *p. 80*

Janet also quotes C.S. Lewis several times. She notes that in his anguish, Lewis called God a "cosmic sadist."

   a. Have you ever spoken about God this way, or wanted to? Share the situation and how you handled it.

   b. Can language like Wolterstorff's or Lewis's be justified? Consider Psalm 88 and Isaiah 55:6-9. How do you imagine God "reacts" to such prayers? (See Romans 8:26-27.) Do we need to be forgiven such prayers?

2. Isaiah writes, "Truly you are a God who hides himself, O God and Savior of Israel" (45:15). In what ways might the Smits feel as if God is hiding from them? Does this verse describe, in any way, how you have experienced God?

3. Lewis writes, "Talk to me about the truth of religion, and I'll listen gladly. Talk to me about the duty of religion, and I'll listen submissively. But don't come talking to me about the consolations of religion, or I shall suspect that you don't understand" (*A Grief Observed*, p. 23). Again, keeping in mind that these words were written shortly after the death of his wife, how do you feel about them?

What about Q & A 1 of the Heidelberg Catechism (see below)? At least in a "feeling way," does this Q & A make less sense sometimes than at other times? Explain.

   Q. *What is your only comfort in life and in death?*

   A. *That I am not my own,
   but belong—
      body and soul,
      in life and in death—
   to my faithful Savior Jesus Christ.*

   *He has fully paid for all my sins with his precious blood,
   and has set me free from the tyranny of the devil.
   He also watches over me in such a way that not a hair can fall from my head without the will of my Father in heaven.*

> *In fact, all things must work together for my salvation.*
>
> *Because I belong to him, Christ, by his Holy Spirit, assures me of eternal life and makes me wholeheartedly willing and ready from now on to live for him.*

4. Share with each other instances in which sin is clearly a power at work in the world and instances in which sin is personal. In what ways are humans responsible for each kind of sin?
5. Reread the conversation between Ralph Smit and Friedrich Konig.
   a. How do you react to an approach like Fred's? How does it make you feel?
   b. Imagine that you overheard Fred's exchange with Mr. Smit and you had an opportunity to speak to Fred pastorally. What would you say? Where would you begin? (See Luke 13:1-9.)
   c. Are there any occasions in which we might be justified in taking Fred's line? For example, what if Ralph had contracted AIDS through a promiscuous homosexual lifestyle? Would it be fair to say that such a disease was a divine punishment? Why or why not?
   d. How should the church respond to such persons: a smoker dying of lung cancer; a homosexual dying of AIDS; a middle-level executive who suffered a stroke from high blood pressure due, in part, to the stresses of her job?
7. Elisabeth Kübler-Ross writes,

   > *In contrast to the stage of denial, this stage of anger is very difficult to cope with from the point of view of family and staff. The reason for this is the fact that this anger is displaced in all directions and projected onto the environment at times almost at random . . . . The problem here is that few people place themselves in the patient's position and wonder where this anger might come from.*
   > —On Death and Dying, pp. 50-51

   Imagine you are an elder or deacon visiting Ralph and you find him angry. What would you try to do or say? Role-play the situation, taking turns assuming the roles of Ralph and the officebearer. Make use of Scripture, if it seems appropriate.

Closing
Close with a hymn of trust in God. "Precious Lord, Take My Hand" (*Psalter Hymnal* 493) and "What a Friend We Have in Jesus" (*Psalter Hymnal* 579; *Rejoice in the Lord* 507) are possible choices. Follow the hymn with a few moments of silent prayer.

THREE

LET'S MAKE A DEAL

May 14, 1990
Dear Diary:
    Miracle of miracles! Dad came home from the hospital last night! His lungs are clear, and the sores in his mouth seem to be under control. He's really tired, and he looks awfully skinny and pale. Still, it's neat to see him sitting in his chair, watching the news. I bought him a new housecoat as a coming-home present, a thick cotton one with a large blue-checkered design. Dad says it's perfect.

May 15, 1990
Dear Diary:
    Danny Prince, our car mechanic, called today. He wants us to visit his new church. He used to go to our church, but it was too old-fashioned for him. There is something to that. Our organist sounds as if she's forever stuck in first gear, and that would turn off a jazzy piano player like Danny.
    Danny's church is called "The Church of the New Vine." They meet in the Odd Fellows Hall. Danny started the church himself with friends—mostly people from our church. They're hooked up with a California denomination that goes for stuff like tongue-speaking and healing.
    Dad says he'll go. I think he agreed partly because the Prince family has been so nice to us. They call every day, they offer us

transportation when we're stuck for rides to the hospital, and they drop off food all the time. But I also think Dad is willing to try anything once. He says a healing service can't be worse than AZT.

May 21, 1990
Dear Diary:
   Last night Dad prayed for healing—like he meant it. But who gets healed from AIDS? I've heard of people with headaches getting healed and of people with insomnia getting healed, but people with AIDS?
   It's weird. Like who would ever pray to get a new arm if he were an amputee? Or who would ever pray for a new breast if she had had a mastectomy? But Danny told Dad that a minister from his denomination went to Australia last year and closed some woman's cleft palate. He said the healing even made some medical journals and that it's all documented. Still . . . I don't expect to see Dad's blood tests come back HIV negative. Dad prayed for it, though. And then he said I had to have faith or maybe it wouldn't work. Dad's almost not normal when he starts talking miracles. It scares me.

May 23, 1990
Dear Diary:
   Today Dad prayed for healing again. This time he told God—right in front of all of us—that if he came back HIV negative, or even if he was still alive and well a year from this coming Christmas (I guess even Dad doesn't have that much faith), he'd quit his job and write a book about what it's like to have AIDS and be healed. Sad thing is that just as he finished his prayer, he had to run from the table because he was sick—from his medicine, I think.

May 27, 1990
Dear Diary:
   Mom and Dad just came home from the Prince's church. Dad's in bed. Mom's crying. The service shook them up, I guess. Mom couldn't even talk about it.
   As I read back over these pages, it's as if the only thing happening in my life is Dad's dying. I should be writing about which college I'm going to (the mail is thick with advertising) or about who I'll go to the dance with. It would be nice to be living just a regular life for a little while. But what's regular?

◆ ◆ ◆

   The service the Smits had last attended was at the Prince home, just out of town, on one of those dirt side roads full of countrified city folk. As Ralph and Diane got out of their car, Danny was already coming down the porch stairs to greet them. Several other cars were in the drive, and another was pulling in. Ralph was surprised to see that it belonged to the Goodwins, another family in their church. In fact, as Ralph looked around, he saw with his trained elder's eye that several of the cars in the driveway belonged, like his own, to stalwart members of his church. What were they all doing here? he wondered.

Danny reached out to the Smits with a hand. "Hey, Ralph. Glad you could make it. Really. This will be good. You'll like it. Hi, Diane!"

"Hi, Danny," said Ralph.

Diane clutched for Ralph's hand. She wanted to know what she and Ralph were doing here. This was just the sort of meeting that Ralph traditionally warned church members against attending. In fact, Ralph had pleaded with Danny just two years ago to reconsider his decision to leave their congregation. Everything was changing too fast. With the way things stood today, taking in a service at Danny's little "sectarian" house church seemed like no big deal. And maybe, just maybe, this group and their prayers could do something for Ralph. But of course, they couldn't. Unless . . . Diane shrunk behind Ralph as Danny spoke.

"Listen, the coffee's on. Everyone's in the family room. Go on in. I'm on greeting duty."

Diane and Ralph went in for coffee. Soon they were making the circuit from one old acquaintance to another. "How are the pig prices, Sam?" and "Nice weather, eh?" and "I wouldn't buy another Renault if they paid me." For a little while, at least, the familiar conversation comforted Ralph and Diane.

Just exactly when the "meeting" started and the visiting stopped was hard to say. Someone picked up a guitar and quietly played some chords. Someone else began to sing along softly—"Lion of Judah." Others joined in, and conversation faltered. Danny announced a song. Soon everyone was singing, and most present had their hands in the air and eyes closed. Ralph and Diane nervously moved closer together on the couch and reached for each other's hand.

After thirty minutes, the music quieted down. Danny picked up a Bible and started reading Acts 3 and 4: Peter and John heal a crippled man. Arrest. Jail. The leaders of the people arrest the two apostles and demand to know, "By what power or what name did you do this?"

Danny stopped. He said, quietly, "Tell me."

Someone said, "Jesus!"

Danny asked again. "By what power or by what name can we do such things?"

"Jesus!" Several people said the name.

"Who?"

"Jesus!" The group was shouting now.

Danny began preaching. His words were as smooth as the car engines he tuned usually ran. He was a good communicator. "Listen! Tell me! By what power or by what name do we live? By Jesus' power. And that power is here today. The Spirit wants us to use that power to do kingdom signs and wonders, to let the world know Jesus reigns! Did you hear about Pastor Smith from California? He was flying somewhere last year when he received a word from the Lord. Pastor Smith saw adultery written on his seatmate's face, and the Lord told him the name of the woman this man was sinning with. Pastor Smith shared this woman's name with his seatmate and told him God didn't approve. And the seatmate—he believed! Changed his ways! By what power, or by what name can such things happen even today?"

"Jesus," came the reply from several people.

"Right," said Danny. "By the name of Jesus, using the shovel of the Spirit. The kingdom of God is real, and it's here among us. You can see it in the miracles. Like when Mr. Goodwin came here in desperation, just a few weeks ago, and shared with us that he was suffering from depression and sadness. And the Lord gave me a word, and it was the name Molash, a demon tormenting brother Goodwin. With prayer we cast Molash out and . . . Peter Goodwin, by what power and by what name did I do this?"

"Jesus!"

"When the people of Israel refused to obey the Lord and were sent into exile, the second sign of God's displeasure, says the psalmist, was that 'We are given no miraculous signs; no prophets are left, and none of us knows how long this will be.' We know. As long as we refuse to claim the power of Jesus' name, we won't have that power. But his kingdom is coming, so let's claim it!"

A chorus of amens followed.

Danny was speaking fast now, with conviction. His eyes were closed, and his hands were clenched. "We have to challenge Jesus' church to claim the power of Jesus' name. The Lord gave me a word. He said 'Danny, go tell it from the mountaintops, go tell it everywhere—but especially, go tell your friends in the old church. Tell them they can claim the power of my name to make the blind see and the lame walk and the deaf hear. Danny, use my name to make cancers disappear and to make hearts beat strong again. Let my world know that my kingdom is here today!'"

Danny slowed down, then, and switched to a more didactic mode. He sipped at a glass of water someone had handed to him. "Jesus demonstrated his kingdom's coming by doing signs and miracles. He healed the sick. He threw out demons. He fed thousands with a few little fish sandwiches. And so did the apostles. I read here in Mark, chapter 1, that he amazed the people with his new teaching—what new teaching? His teaching that even the evil spirits obey him. And if we are his vessels, those evil spirits will obey him still, through us.

"Look, I'm not saying God is going to heal all our diseases now. Of course not. But God wants to use us to announce that a day is coming when he will heal all our diseases and make all things new. Not everyone who comes here for healing is going to get it. But lots of people who come here claiming the power of God will be healed. So the world will have a little taste now of what heaven is going to be like. That's what happened with the crippled beggar at the temple gate. When he started walking and dancing and praising the Lord, he thought he was in heaven, and who can blame him? The priests and the temple guard—they knew that something awesome had happened too. That's why they asked Peter and John, 'By what power or what name did you do this?' Friends, let's claim that power. Now! Let's raise our hands in prayer. Let's slay Baal's prophets with fire from heaven! Now! Let's damn the devils and fly with the Spirit and go sail into Jesus' kingdom come. Now!"

Someone stood up, then, and shouted out, "Ralph Smit! Ralph Smit! I have a word for Ralph Smit. You're sick! Sick with a terrible disease. It's not your fault. But God wants you to claim the Spirit! He wants you healed. He wants you to do kingdom work for ten more years. Then you're on your own again. Ten years. Stand up, Ralph."

Ralph stood up, shaking, sweating. What else was there to do? Danny came over and asked Ralph if he really wanted to be delivered from his disease.

"Yes."

"For ten years?"

"Yes," said Ralph.

"You got it," said Danny. "But you have to pray. We all have to pray. Your family too. You have to believe in the power of the kingdom. You have to claim the power of Jesus' name!" Four or five people started talking unintelligibly, loudly, right through Danny. A woman was crying somewhere. Ralph was crying. A guitar was playing "Magnify the Lord."

Danny and Peter Goodwin put their hands on Ralph and Diane and prayed. "Heal Ralph, God, because he needs to know how it feels to be made newer than new, because this disease is eating him up, because his neighbors want to see you in splendor and majesty. Please, God, hear our prayers." This went on for fifteen or twenty minutes, through music and tongue-speaking and hand-holding and others' praying in the corners.

Finally, Danny sat Ralph down again. The singing kept up for another few minutes, and then, slowly, one by one, people began to leave. Ralph and Diane got up. Danny whispered, "Give me a call, Ralph, tomorrow." Then Danny stood up and asked for quiet. "Let's pray," he said, and Danny prayed a prayer of thanksgiving. "Thank you, God, for offering Ralph deliverance from AIDS. Help Ralph to claim it, Lord, so that he and all of us may see and believe that Jesus' name and power are real. Thank you for showing us how to take on the dark forces of evil and beat them back. Amen." With that, Ralph and Diane walked out into the dark yard, slid into the car, and somehow found their way home.

Danny dropped by several times over the next few days to pray for healing. And for a few days, Ralph said he definitely felt better. He spoke with Diane again about quitting his job and getting a word processor. But then . . . Diane began to notice a wheezing in his breath. "A little cold," said Ralph, but he looked afraid. "My first cold since healing."

Later that night, gasping for air, Ralph was taken to the hospital. Pneumocytosis again, said the doctor. The prognosis was not good.

◆ ◆ ◆

June 4, 1990
Dear Manny:
It's tough being so far apart after growing so close together at seminary. How are things? I hope you managed to straighten out that car allowance mix-up. Sounds like your administration committee wants to do the right thing, but they're just not sure how.

Things over here are going pretty well. A lot has happened to that member of my congregation who has AIDS. I want to share it with you in the hope that writing it down will help me think things through.

Ralph, the man with AIDS, is a stalwart guy: dependable, supportive, neat family, etc., etc. Over the past few months, as I've gone through this thing with Ralph, I've also "fallen in love" with him as a brother in Christ. Somehow, through the crisis of this thing, the barriers between us have fallen, and we relate really well.

Well, a pastor from a neighboring church called me last week and asked if I knew that Ralph had been out to "the Prince place." I said I didn't know and that I had never heard of "the Prince place." Well, the caller filled me in.

Apparently Danny Prince was a member of one of the CRC churches here in town—but not a very happy member. He started church hopping, to see if there was a better place for him and his musical gifts. Eventually, he got involved with the "Church of the New Vine," which is growing like wildfire. That church's theology is rooted in the "kingdom" theology of George Eldon Ladd, and so it has something in it that really resonates with our Reformed instincts. The twist at New Vine is that since the kingdom is here now, the signs and wonders that accompanied Christ's ministry ought to be here too. This church emphasizes its healing ministry as a showplace for seeing that Jesus' kingdom has arrived in power. They lean heavily toward other charismatic practices too, although they reject a second "Holy Spirit" baptism.

As it turns out, Ralph went to one of their services and got himself healed of his AIDS for ten years, apparently. Except that he's in the hospital again, as sick as ever and feeling like a fool to boot.

When I next visited Ralph, he was right up front, as usual. It turns out that he made a deal with God, in the most blatant way. He promised God that if he was healed of AIDS for even a little while, he would write a book about his experience. Kübler-Ross would call this the "bargaining" stage in learning to deal with death.

You can't blame Ralph, of course. Life is a precious gift to us from God, and Ralph won't give it up easily. But I was sad to see how Ralph's desire for life led him down a path that he himself had so often and so loudly insisted was a wrong turn. Ralph knew it and was ashamed of his inconsistent behavior. So we talked about it.

What Ralph really wanted to know was whether it was wrong for him to pray for healing from AIDS. I said, "No, it's not." Now I'm trying to sort out my thoughts on miracles at greater length, so I'm writing them out here, in order. Please feel free to respond to them.

First, it seems very important to me that we are sure what we are talking about when we say "miracle." Too many people, eager to experience "God" in a miracle, forget to see their Lord and Creator anywhere else. But just because we have come to bank on the world spinning around the sun, or on the surgeon cutting out an appendix, is no reason to think that God is any less involved in these sorts of things than in what we classify as "miracles." I like how Lewis Smedes put it in his little Ministry and the Miraculous:

> In the biblical view, a miracle is a signal that God is, for a moment and for a special purpose, walking down paths he does not usually walk. A miracle is not a sign that a God who is usually absent is, for the moment, present. It is only a sign that God who is always present in creative power is working here and now in an unfamiliar style.
>
> —pp. 48-49

Augustine defines miracles similarly. "A portent . . . happens not contrary to nature, but contrary to what we know as nature" (De civitate Dei, XII.8).

Second, throughout salvation history miracles always seem to have been a "here today, gone tomorrow" sort of phenomenon. In the Bible, there were times when lots of miracles happened—during the Exodus, for example, or during Elijah and Elisha's day, or during Christ's ministry. Miracles also seem to have played an important role in the early history of the church and on the mission field. On the other hand, at other times there have been very few miracles among God's people—during the age of the patriarchs, for example, or in the times both before and after the exile, or in our time, in the West, since the Enlightenment.

Third, the New Testament makes it plain that miracles are not going to be the Christian's ticket out of suffering in and with the rest of the world. We still long for the time when healing is whole and death is no more, says John (Rev. 21:4). We pray the Lord's Prayer precisely because the kingdom has not yet come with all its promised shalom. The New Testament returns time and again to the theme that we as Christians need to prepare ourselves for suffering, for carrying crosses, for persecutions, for self-denial, and for a groaning with all the rest of our hurting creation (Rom. 8:22). Paul says, "To this very hour we go hungry and thirsty, we are in rags, we are brutally treated, we are homeless (1 Cor. 4:11). Paul also seems to suggest in 2 Corinthians 12:12 that miracles are, primarily at least, the province of apostles.

Fourth, Jesus didn't like it when the crowds wanted him to do miracles to prove something about himself. "A wicked and adulterous generation asks for a miraculous sign!" (Matt. 12:39, 16:4). He regretted it when people wanted him to prove that he was the Messiah (Luke 11:16; John 4:48). The apostle Paul, in the same spirit, identified a desire for signs as characteristic not of faith but of Jewish skepticism about Jesus (1 Cor. 1:22).

Fifth, when I think of Danny Prince, I can't help remembering an article I read last year in Psychology Today. It was entitled "The New Spirituality: Healing Rituals Hit the Suburbs" (Jan./Feb. 1989), and it described how healing miracles are a big hit these days not only among Christians but also among a whole range of other groups, including those involved in New Age thinking, the Occult, Eastern religions, and folk-medicine. One of the themes of the article was that mysticism has gone mainstream. All sorts of people these days seem to want a personal god-connection and a warm-fuzzy community to belong to. Is Danny Prince offering his miracles to satiate the unique demands of this new kind of religious consumer?

What troubles me about the Prince ministry, I suppose, is that miracles are so central to its public face. Even though Danny himself would never claim to be able to get God to do miracles at will, and even though Danny often says more people leave his services unhealed than healed, his ministry leaves the strong impression that miracles and other sorts of special pipelines from God to his group are the "main event." And the fact of the matter is that even though Danny plans on God not answering all his prayers for healing, he is not well equipped to handle the sort of thing that happened to Ralph. Danny deals in success, not failure. Now that it's clear Ralph is really sick again, Danny has dropped out of sight as far as the Smit family is concerned.

All in all, there seems to be a basic unwillingness in society at large, including our churches, to confront suffering as suffering. Probably one of the main parts of our jobs as ministers should be to enable our parishioners to deal with suffering until all things are made new. So we have to concentrate on showing our parishioners Jesus and on passing along to them the attitude of Jesus (Phil. 2:5-11).

Often it has been the artists among us who are best able to express what Jesus' compassion is all about. For example, C.S. Lewis describes the compassion of Jesus by portraying it in Aslan, a huge lion of Judah, a lion that rules the land of Narnia. You only need to look at Aslan to know how dangerous he is. He is huge, twice as large as any other lion, and he's fierce in battle, mighty beyond words. It takes courage to come before Aslan, for he can strike you down with his breath if he has a mind to. But a little boy named Digory screws up his courage anyway; he walks up to Aslan with head bowed and asks him to please heal his mother, whom he loves. "Please, please—won't you—can't you give me something that will cure Mother?" asks Digory.

Aslan, the Jesus of Narnia, is quiet after Digory's prayer. So Digory lifts his eyes and dares a short glance at Aslan's face to see what the lion will do.

> What [Digory] saw surprised him as much as anything in his whole life. For [Aslan's] tawny face was bent down near his own and (wonder of wonders) great shining tears stood in the Lion's eyes. They were such big, bright tears compared with Digory's own that for a moment he felt as if the Lion must really be sorrier about his Mother than he was himself.
>
> —*The Magician's Nephew;* Macmillan, 1955; p. 142

Compassion. The tears of God. The pain God feels with us and for us.

So all in all, should we ask for miracles today? Sure. But let's make sure we ask for them in some kind of faithful relation to what really ails this world. I think Lewis Smedes got it right when he wrote,

> My problem [with miracles] was a nagging anxiety I felt about touting miraculous healings of assorted bearable ailments as signals of God's power and God's desire to heal our suffering in a world chock-full of suffering that never comes close to getting healed. It was a feeling I could not shake . . . a feeling about the fittingness, even the decency, of celebrating far and wide the miraculous healing of a relatively few ailments within a world endemically infected by enormous, intractable, unalleviated suffering. It felt to me like proclaiming that God is alive and well in the world because you survived an airplane crash in which everyone else perished. And proclaiming your personal joy to those who mourned their dead.
>
> So I wonder how we can appropriately celebrate the miraculous healings of sick people in a world of chronic and unhealed pain?
> —"Of Miracles and Suffering," The Reformed Journal, Feb. 1989, pp. 14-21

Well, Manny, I'm at the end of this letter with the very question I began with. Should we pray for miracles? Sure. But let's pray for miracles in some kind of proper proportion to what really ails this world. It isn't Ralph's AIDS so much as people's unbelief that needs healing, and it isn't someone's cleft palate that is critical so much as the injustices in our health-care system—not to mention the incredible injustice of no health care for most people in developing nations.

Do miracles still happen today? I suppose so. In fact, I'm sure of it. Just listen to our missionaries describe the battle between Satan's minions and Jesus' church in much of the nonindustrialized world. And don't forget Ralph's wife, Diane. She doesn't test positive for HIV. It's a miracle, of course, but not the sort of miracle God intends to use to make a big splash in the world (though it has certainly made a splash with Diane, her family, and their doctor).

And what about Danny Prince and his group? They are brothers and sisters, of course, in Jesus Christ. In most things they are very close to us. My prayer for them is that their hankering after miracles won't sidetrack them from the main thing they, or any church, is called to—being ambassadors of reconciliation. And I hope our skepticism of and for Prince's kind of miracles is born more out of an honest struggle to discern how the Spirit wants us to confront the powers and principalities of this age than out of a fear or distaste for the unusual or emotional or new.

Looking forward to your response,
Lewis Venema

Suggestions for Group Session

Opening

Read Mark 7:31-8:13, an account of two miracles that Jesus performed during his ministry. You may also wish to sing "Your Hands, O Lord, in Days of Old" (*Psalter Hymnal* 363) or "Come, You Disconsolate" (*Psalter Hymnal* 538; *Trinity Hymnal* 615).

For Discussion

1. Have you ever experienced healing or come into contact with someone who was healed miraculously? Share the experience with the group.

2. Have churches that offered healing services in your community had an impact on your own church's membership? If so, why? Does this speak to a shortcoming in your church, to the doctrinal errors of those who left, or to a combination of the two? Defend your answer.

3. Danny Prince accounts for the presence of God's healing power by saying that if the kingdom is present, then its power ought to be plain to see. Is Danny right? What other shapes might the presence of God's kingdom take in the life of the Christian community? Try to answer the question in terms of both personal and collective action that members of your Christian community can engage in.

4. At one point, Danny tells Ralph that his part in the miracle is that "he has to pray." If Ralph isn't healed, what might the effect of such a statement have on him?

5. Divide into four groups, with each group taking the role of one of the main characters: Danny, Janet, Ralph, and Lew Venema. How would each answer the question "Ought we to pray for healing?" Be ready to support your conclusions.

6. Elisabeth Kübler-Ross describes the bargaining phase of encountering death when she writes,

> *If we have been unable to face the sad facts in the first period [denial], and have been angry at people and God in the second phase, maybe we can succeed in entering into some sort of an agreement which may postpone the inevitable happening . . . . The bargaining is really an attempt to postpone; it has to include a prize offered "for good behavior." It also sets a self-imposed "deadline," and it includes an implicit promise that the patient will not ask for more if this one postponement is granted.*
>
> —On Death and Dying, pp. 82-84

How does Ralph fit this description? To dying people who go through a stage of bargaining, what is the danger of Danny's kind of ministry?

7. Many modern churches subscribe to the "religious supermarket" model through which they compete with other churches for bigger membership by offering a larger and more desirable smorgasbord of spiritual products that hopefully meet the "needs" of the religious consumer. Does Danny's church fall into that sort of model by offering "healing"? Is this an appropriate model for the church to operate on to any degree? To what extent ought churches to consider what people think they need as opposed, perhaps, to what they really need?

8. Reread what Lewis Smedes has to say about personal miracles in light of "what really ails this world," especially his remarks about the person who survives an airplane crash. Discuss. Is Smedes onto something here? Should whatever he is getting at stop us from praying for healing altogether? Why or why not?

Closing

Make up a list of concerns that exist in today's world—locally and globally—and pray for them in some kind of proportion to what really ails the world. Do the same for a list of things for which your group ought to give thanksgiving. Take turns praying for these items.

FOUR

TOO TIRED TO SMILE

February 13, 1991
Dear Diary,
   Dad is back in the hospital again. It's the fourth time since June. He's not doing very well. He has an oxygen tube under his nose all the time now, and he gets blood every third or fourth day because of his anemia. He coughs a lot and complains about his swollen glands. AIDS hurts. Dad still likes to talk, but he doesn't make you feel like you have to talk when you're there. That's good, because mostly I hardly know what to say.
   I'm really worried about Mom these days too. She doesn't take care of herself. She'll wear the same dress to the hospital two or three times in a week, so by Friday it's stained and crumpled. She doesn't even seem to notice! She is also getting sloppy with her makeup. When I mentioned it to her last night, she said she didn't care. Today she wasn't even wearing any.

February 14, 1991
Dear Diary,
   Tomorrow I have a big physics test. It covers everything we've studied since Christmas break. I haven't studied for it at all. I just can't get up for it.
   Usually Dad cracked the whip for me when it came to physics. He said it was fun to be able to tell me a thing or two and not get an argument. He sure had a knack for going through it so that I under-

stood the material. But this is all past tense. I'm going to flunk the test, I guess.

February 15, 1991
Dear Diary,
    I skipped my test. Mr. De Waal saw me afterwards, and I thought he was going to go for my jugular, but he just shrugged his shoulders and said we could reschedule it.
    It's interesting how people treat us now. Some just ignore us because they don't know what to say. That's the worst. No, it's even worse when they don't ignore you but never bring it up. It's like Dad's dying is the forbidden topic. That feels very lonely.
    The best is when people make it a point to ask me how Dad is or how the family is doing. Mr. De Waal is like that. I can't be real honest with him, because I get too upset. But at least I know he's thinking (and praying, he says) about us.
    Church friends have been great. We have two years' worth of soup and buns and lasagna and pound cake in the freezer. Most people just stop by with their food and then leave quickly. That helps. We need our space. The church bulletin had an announcement asking people to visit Dad only during visiting hours because he's feeling weak. For the most part people have stuck to that. That helps, because it means we have private time with Dad in the hospital.

February 20, 1991
Dear Diary,
    Harry asked me out. There's a Cowboy Junkie concert in London on Friday. I'd love to go, but I promised Mom I'd visit Dad on Friday night so that she could stay home. So I said no. Just as well, I guess. Harry seems nice, but I don't think I can do the work a first date requires right now.
    When I visited Dad this afternoon, Rev. Venema was just getting set to read the Bible. I looked up the passage he read (Isa. 43:1-5) and am writing it down here so that I'll never forget it. "But now, this is what the LORD says—he who created you, Janet, he who formed you, Ralph [yes, the minister changed the words]: 'Fear not, for I have redeemed you; I have summoned you by name; you are mine. When you pass through the waters ["as you are now," said the minister], I will be with you; and when you pass through the rivers, they will not sweep over you. When you walk through the fire, you will not be burned; the flames will not set you ablaze . . . . Do not be afraid, for I am with you . . . .'" I needed those words, because I'm depressed. It's nice to hear that one of the things God

does is suffer through the tough times with you. It helps you not to feel so guilty about being down.

Another hard thing is that we're studying portions of Dante's Divine Comedy *in English class. Not only is it almost impossible to read, but the subject matter is sometimes almost impossible for me to talk about. Dante describes getting lost in the woods, where lions and leopards block his way out. An ancient poet by the name of Virgil finds Dante and offers to show him the way out, but it means going through purgatory, hell, and heaven.*

So it turns out that just as I begin to wonder about these things, Mr. Hull is teaching us about them in religion class, in sync with the English class (cooperative teaching is all the rage these days). I would have run out of his class in tears at least three or four times by now, but I don't want everyone to see me so upset. I guess I have to learn to look those things straight in the face. There's a religion test tomorrow, and this time I'm going through with it. I'll have to try to study in the hospital. Dad will probably be sleeping anyway.

◆ ◆ ◆

When Janet arrived at the hospital, a tape of last Sunday morning's sermon was playing. Her father's eyes were closed, though, and Janet wasn't really sure if he was awake. The tape was past the sermon, and the congregation was singing "All Things Bright and Beautiful." Janet entered through the harsh sun of the late afternoon, sat down in a chair, pulled out her notes, and began reading.

Dante and Virgil began their adventure on the uppermost slopes of hell. In the Middle Ages, before the Reformation, most people thought hell was as Dante described it—a place that had nine levels of suffering. The higher up you were, the less suffering you did. In the top level of hell, limbo, lived those good and virtuous pagans who had never been baptized: Homer the poet, Plato the philosopher, and Hippocrates the doctor. The deepest level of hell was reserved for people who betrayed friends, family, or church—people such as Brutus, who murdered Julius Caesar, and, of course, Judas, who betrayed Jesus. These traitors were all frozen in ice.

Mr. Hull said that many people—mostly those who hadn't given the matter much thought and who hadn't gone to the Bible for guidance—still thought hell was something like that. Janet supposed that she did too—at least the parts about fire and torment and demons. The ice was a new touch, though.

As Janet read over her notes, her father was waking to the soft monotone of his tape run to an end. He quietly observed his daughter for a while. Finally he spoke. "Hi, sweetheart. Can you let down the blinds, please? The sun gets to my eyes." Janet got up and closed the blinds. "You here again, Janet?"

"Dad." A hint of loving consternation. "I always visit you."

"I don't know why. Don't you get sick of it?"

"Dad! You're starting to sound like Mom. Lately all she talks about is how she isn't doing enough for you and how stupid she feels for not being sick when you are."

"Well, I'm not sure how long she can keep it up. I'm not sure how long I can keep it up either. Sometimes I think I should just get it over with and die. No more IVs, no more oxygen, no more blood, no more medicine. I can't be nice company for you. I can barely concentrate on the sermons I get. I'm always hungry, but I never want to eat. I hardly keep track of time. I fall asleep constantly."

"Dad?" Janet had a big pit in her stomach. Was this her father? The man who used to laugh as much as he breathed, almost—who ran around the house talking in nursery rhymes to his kids and grandkids? Was this the man who listened to her whenever she needed someone to talk to, who gave advice only when she asked for it (well, mostly only then), who sang songs doing the dishes? He scared her now.

"Janet, I cry every day. I can't help it. I'm sick of it."

"I don't know what to say, Dad. I just love you."

"I don't know why you come all the time. But I'm glad. I guess I just feel sad. And who can blame me? I'll try to put on a better face for a while." A tear was gathering in the corner of his eye. "What are you studying?"

"Religion. We have a test tomorrow."

"But what exactly? You have to tell me so that I can get my mind off this." Ralph nodded vaguely at the room.

"Well, um . . ." Janet decided she'd better not be the one who avoided all mention of embarrassing or difficult subjects. "I'm studying about hell, purgatory, and heaven. Not exactly the kind of stuff that's much fun to talk about."

"We'll do it. We'll brave the sea. Do you have a review sheet? Give it to me, and I'll go through it with you. I feel wide awake now anyway. I've slept most of the afternoon, and now I have a headache." Janet handed him a paper. "First question," said her father. "What did the Old Testament Israelites believe happened after persons died?"

"Do you really want to go through this, Dad?" Her father tried to smile and nodded his head. Janet noticed his arms. He was as thin as a rail.

"Well, then, in the Old Testament, people believed that after they died, they went to a place called *Sheol*. The dead in Sheol are called . . . I don't remember."

"The *rephaim*, variously translated as 'the dead,' as in Psalm 88:10, or 'the spirits of the departed,' as in Isaiah 14:9."

"Right, the rephaim. I don't have to memorize all those text references. Anyway, Sheol wasn't like hell, really, because it was a place where both Jew and non-Jew went when they died, whether they were good or bad. In Sheol, people have a kind of ghostly, sleepy, and lethargic life—though it's not really life, of course . . ."

"You have a whole list of texts here: Job 3:13; Ecclesiastes 9:10; Isaiah 38:18; Psalms 88:10-12, 115:17-18."

"Right . . . but anyway, in Sheol, every once in a while, people were able to get up and do things. For example, Samuel was called up out of Sheol by the Witch of Endor, and he warned Saul that soon he and his son Jonathan would join him. People in Sheol don't have their earthly bodies, of course, but they do seem to have something like a body—Samuel, for example, appeared to the Witch of Endor wearing clothes."

"Anything else?" asked her dad, looking up from the question sheet for a minute, intrigued.

"Well, one thing more. There are hints in the Old Testament that Sheol is not the last and only resting place for the good. We had to memorize Psalm 49:15, 'God will redeem my soul from the grave; he will surely take me to himself.' There's a passage from Isaiah too, but I don't know it."

"'But your dead will live; their bodies will rise. You who dwell in the dust, wake up and shout for joy. Your dew is like the dew of the morning; the earth will give birth to her dead,'" Ralph read from Janet's notes. "Isaiah 26:19."

"Right. I memorized the short one. All in all, what the Old Testament says about Sheol makes it plain that between our dying and the resurrection people are in an 'intermediate state' where the soul lives on without the body. The New Testament tells us a bit more about what that intermediate state between death and resurrection is like." Janet tried to smile, but the topic was too close to home.

"Well, what does the New Testament say about the dead?" asked Ralph. "It's funny, you know, but I haven't heard many sermons on this topic. I never really thought about it that much. My impression is that when I die, I'll go to be with Jesus. But on the other hand, I won't be with Jesus in the flesh. How can I? I won't have my resurrection body yet. What does Mr. Hull say, Janet?"

"Well, Mr. Hull says that when we die, we go to be with the Lord—just as the thief on the cross did—but that until the final judgment, only our souls will be with Jesus. It's that whole thing about the intermediate state again. To help us understand it better, Mr. Hull had us memorize Lord's Day 22 from the Heidelberg Catechism. The first question and answer in that Lord's Day, Q & A 57, is really about the resurrection of the body but says something about us before the resurrection too. It says the resurrection comforts us because, 'Not only my soul will be taken immediately after this life to Christ its head, but even my very flesh, raised by the power of Christ, will be reunited with my soul and made like Christ's glorious body.' I don't remember the Bible passages."

"You list Philippians 1:21-23 and 2 Corinthians 5:8."

"Right, but we don't have to memorize those. Basically, when we die, we go to heaven to be with Jesus. And being with Jesus, even if it isn't as nice as being with him on the new earth, is really wonderful."

"And what about those who are not 'with Jesus'? What happens to them before the judgment and resurrection?"

"That's a very hard question to answer, Dad. There's only one passage in the Bible that talks about someone in the intermediate state who is not in God's good grace. That's the parable of Lazarus and the rich man. And it's very dangerous to draw too many conclusions from this parable about the intermediate state, because that's not the focus of the story; the parable is really about the danger of riches and not loving your neighbor. Maybe Jesus was just using popular myths about the afterlife as a setting for his parable. Still, in this parable, the dead rich man wants to warn his family to shape up before they die, so that they don't suffer after death like he is suffering."

"Just a few questions to go, Janet. What does the New Testament say about hell?"

"Not much, really, though what the Bible says is not all that comfortable. In short, hell is a place where evil people who have not relied on Jesus for salvation go after dying. The Bible uses words like fire, darkness, sulfur, and smoke (Matt. 13:41-42, 22:13; Mark 9:48; Rev. 14:10-11) to describe hell, and it says those in hell will weep and gnash their teeth. John Calvin did not take these descriptions literally; he called them metaphors and said the Bible uses them to give us some idea of how awful it is to be cut off from all fellowship with God (Institutes, III.xxv.12). I think I covered the main things we're supposed to know."

"Why is the New Testament picture of what happens at death different from the Old Testament picture? What happened to Sheol?"

"A lot of kids wanted to know that. Mr. Hull said most people don't read their Bible closely enough to notice these sorts of discrepancies. He said there were two basic ways of handling them. First, you have to remember that the Bible writers were not newspaper reporters. That kind of writing wasn't invented until about two hundred years ago, so you can't hold biblical writers to those kind of standards.

"Second, we have a doctrine of 'progressive revelation.' I don't understand it very well, but what it adds up to is that God didn't reveal everything that could be known about heaven and hell all at once. Genesis offers a less complete picture of the afterlife than Isaiah does, for example. That means that sometimes the writers of the Psalms reflect only a hazy notion about what will happen when people die—just as they sometimes reflect incomplete notions about the Messiah."

"Good. One more thing. What about purgatory?"

"Well, when Christians die, they go to be with the Lord. We've covered that. But some people—Roman Catholics, for example—think that the intermediate state might be a time of cleansing from sin. They get their doctrine from 1 Corinthians 3, where Paul writes . . . I don't remember the exact words. You have them there. Will you read them?"

"Paul says, 'If any man builds on [the foundation of Jesus Christ] using gold, silver, costly stones, wood, hay or straw, his work will be shown for what it is because the Day will bring it to light. It will be revealed with fire, and the fire will test the quality of each man's work. If what he has built survives, he will receive his reward. If it is burned up, he will suffer loss; he himself will be saved, but only as one escaping through the flames.'"

Janet continued. "According to Roman Catholics, purgatory turns out to be where some people escape the wrath of God only as one escaping through flames. Let's see." Janet closed her eyes, trying to remember what more there was to say. "The doctrine of purgatory is related to the way Roman Catholics pray for the dead. There's this passage in 2 Maccabees where the commander of the forces of Israel sent thousands of drachmas of silver to Jerusalem so that sacrifices could be offered for the sins of the dead. Catholics say that this passage proves prayers for the dead make sense."

"Does it?"

"Only if you think that Maccabees is the inspired Word of God, and we don't; and even then, just because someone in the Bible does something, it doesn't mean that he or she was right in doing it. For example, just because in Acts the first Christians sold everything and gave it to the poor, doesn't mean we have to."

Janet, for all her embarrassment with discussing the material in class, had become very interested in it and had studied hard. She continued on with the facts, in a monotone, looking at the ceiling. The sun had passed behind some clouds, and the room was turning very dark. "Jesus says in Matthew 12:32 that 'anyone who speaks against the Holy Spirit will not be forgiven . . . in this age or in the age to come.' Catholics argue that it would be silly for Jesus to say that some sins could not be forgiven in the life to come unless some sins were actually forgiven there—and that would be purgatory again. St. Augustine says the same thing in the *City of God*.

"But really, if there is a purgatory, the Bible doesn't say anything about it. What Mr. Hull says over and over when he talks about purgatory and hell is this: on the last day, the day of judgment, what is going to surprise us is the mercy and love of God. He thinks the Bible says 'Judge not, that you will not be judged' mostly because humans have never learned how to judge mercifully—only God can really do that right." Janet paused, then noticed that her father was sleeping.

◆ ◆ ◆

When Ralph Smit woke again, the room was dark. Janet was gone. "Someone will probably come after supper," he thought. He thought about Janet's test. He thought about dying. He had always imagined himself dying of a heart attack. Weak hearts ran in his family. Somehow, a weak heart was a lot easier to understand than AIDS. Hearts had to push five quarts of blood through more than sixty thousand miles of blood vessels and capillaries by pumping sixty or seventy times a minute. No wonder people died from heart attacks. It would have suited him at least, he thought grimly.

Janet had not wanted to talk about hell and purgatory or even about heaven. She thought it would upset him. She was right. But not for the reason she thought—not because he didn't want to think about dying. He did. He wanted to know everything he could about dying and what happened next. It was very relevant to him now.

The talk had upset him because he had some fears about what would happen to him, in particular, when he died. Sometimes he worried that even though he had escaped having a heart attack, he might not escape having a faith attack.

What if his spiritual heart gave out under the stress of these days? What would happen then? He was in pain now, but what if it got worse and worse and finally, unlike Job (Ralph was no Job, and he knew it), he cursed God and died? He had been having doubts lately. He didn't feel at peace with dying.

Ralph knew that Arminius, the great bogeyman of his church's past, had seemed to suggest that this was possible. Arminius had been a great Amsterdam preacher who was also—at least according to the writer of one study guide he remembered—greatly mistaken. He taught that true believers not only could but also actually did fall from faith sometimes. Arminius believed in faith attacks, and he believed they could be fatal. Ralph did not like the feel of that. It worried him. He knew he was no saint.

Ralph thought miserably about some of the elder's visits he had made to the old-age home during his last term. He had been shocked at how many of them there—people who had given every appearance of having lived saintly lives for seventy or eighty years, who had been in church twice every Sunday their whole lives—spoke fearfully about what lay on the other side of the grave for them. They worried that they were not good enough to get into heaven. Right or wrong, their hearts condemned them. Ralph had wondered about this when he saw such people, and he had passed it off to their old-fashioned Calvinist upbringing. But now, finally, Ralph knew how they felt. Oh, how glib his answers had been before.

Ralph made a little checklist. He had some skeletons in his closet. He had never actually cheated on his wife—nor had he ever intended to. But he had flirted with his secretaries and had once even had to explain to a secretary that he was not serious. She had quit soon after and had been cold to him until she was gone. She had charged him with using her and with lying. He saw now that there had been some truth to her charges.

Then there were his kids. He felt he had really messed up there sometimes—left it all to Mom. He had been gone too many nights, too many weeks on end, on sales trips. When he was home, he spent too much time at church and school, always needing to be busy, never really learning how to nurture those near to him. He felt as if he had been a distant father.

Then there was his slothful streak. Sure, he looked busy out there. But he had spent a lot of his time lethargically staring at the wall; too often he had waited until the last minute, under pressure, to whip it all together. When other people thought he was busy, he was often relaxing with a paper and a cup of coffee. His business trips had been good excuses to "veg out" during the afternoons in his hotel, with the television and a novel.

Was he good enough? Had he really given his all over to Jesus? He had not.

One part of him said that none of this really mattered, because he had been saved by grace, not works. But in his chest, he was feeling the cramps and pains of guilt, of a faith attack.

When Ralph saw Sister St. John passing in the hallway, he buzzed the nurses' station and asked for her. She came a few minutes later and greeted him warmly, holding his hand in both of hers. Then she pulled up a chair and sat down as close to him as she could. Ralph had come to like this woman. She knew how to listen, long and patiently. She didn't sermonize. She—well, she just ministered. Ralph told her what he had been thinking. He told her he was embarrassed by his thoughts, but not embarrassed enough to stop thinking them.

As was her custom, Sister St. John was quiet for a long time. Then she asked Ralph what he used to say to the doubting elderly he visited.

"Well, I'd remind them about the Canons of Dort, mostly. That's one of our church's confessions. The Canons teach a doctrine called the perseverance of the saints. I'd tell these old people that the Canons teach that their effort to do good works and their bad conscience about failing are proof that the Holy Spirit is still at work in their hearts. So they don't have to worry that they're not elect. The Canons put great store in texts such as, 'I give [my sheep] eternal life, and they shall never perish; no one can snatch them out of my hand'" (John 10:28).

Sister St. John listened to Ralph for a while. Then she said, "It sounds to me like you're on the right track. I think that before you die, you'll realize it too. It will be my prayer for you, tonight, in chapel. Can I tell you a story?"

Ralph nodded.

"Before my father died, in the early seventies, he had had two heart attacks over the course of five years or so. While he was recovering from his first heart attack, he discovered what other heart patients sometimes discover: heart medication can have minor, but disturbing, hallucinogenic side effects. Usually the doctors can adjust the medication so that eventually the side effects can be eliminated, or at least controlled.

"My father seemed to be prone to hallucinations, especially when he was relaxing. He would suddenly begin to think unkind or unholy thoughts that he couldn't rid himself of. He suffered tremendous guilt on account of it. Sometimes he even felt lost to God. While it lasted, it was awful. He told the doctors (he had that much sense), and over the course of several months they were finally able to set things straight. Still, while it lasted, his faith was sorely tried.

"One thing my father did to control his hallucinating was to concentrate. He would pick up his Bible and read. So you must imagine him for a minute, worried and upset at this turn his life had taken, full of drug-induced but very real doubts about faith and salvation, recovering from a heart attack, Bible open on his lap. What he read was this promise from 1 John 3: 'This then is how we know that we belong to the truth, and how we set our hearts at rest in his presence whenever our hearts condemn us. For God is greater than our hearts, and he knows everything.'

"Those words were a revelation to my father. 'God is greater than our hearts.' That promise cut right through his troubles and really comforted him.

"Those words can be a comfort for you too, Ralph, when you wonder if you have the strength to make it. The truth of the matter is that you don't have the strength. But God does. He is greater than your heart. The psalmist promised that the lovingkindness of the Lord is from eternity to eternity. Paul promised us that nothing in all creation will be able to separate us from the love of God in Christ. Jesus himself said, 'I give [my sheep] eternal life and they shall never perish; no one can snatch them out of my hand.' We believe that after going through the trouble of rescuing us from sin, God won't let go of us again. Even if we are weak, we can set our hearts at rest . . . for God is greater than our hearts."

Sister St. John sat and prayed silently, while Ralph looked up at the ceiling. After a while, a smile came over his face, and he closed his eyes. Sister St. John adjusted his sheets and left.

Suggestions for Group Session

Opening

Read the account of the final judgment in Revelation 20:11-15.

As a group, you may want to confess together the words of the following section of *Our World Belongs to God*, a contemporary testimony of the Christian Reformed Church:

> We long for that day
> when Jesus will return as triumphant king,
> when the dead will be raised
> and all people will stand before his judgment.
> We face that day without fear,
> for the Judge is our Savior.
> Our daily lives of service aim for the moment
> when the Son will present his people to the Father.
> Then God will be shown to be true, holy, and gracious.
> All who have been on the Lord's side
> will be honored,
> the fruit of even small acts of
> obedience will be displayed;
> but tyrants and oppressors,
> heretics, and all who deny the Lord
> will be damned.
>
> *—stanza 57*

For Discussion

1. Two Catholic theologians, Thomas and Gertrude Sartory, are quoted by Hans Kung in his *Eternal Life?*. They say,

   > No religion in the world (not a single one in the history of humanity) has on its conscience so many millions of people who thought differently, believed differently. Christianity is the most murderous religion there has ever been. Christians today have to live with this, they have to "overcome" this sort of past. And the real cause of this perversion of the Christian spirit is "belief in hell." If someone is convinced that God condemns a person to hell for all eternity for no other reason than because he is a heathen, a Jew or a heretic, he cannot for his own part fail to regard all heathens, Jews and heretics as good for nothing, as unfit to exist and unworthy of life. Seen from this standpoint, the almost complete extermination of the North and South American Indians by the "Christian" conquerors is quite consistent. From the aspect of the dogma of hell, "baptism or death" is an understandable motto.
   >
   > —Eternal Life? New York: Doubleday, 1984; p. 132.

   a. Is the Sartory argument believable?
   b. How should the doctrine of hell function in our theology?
   c. Richard Mouw says, "A denial of hell often goes hand in hand with a minimizing of the fact of human sin" ("The Waning of Hell," *The Banner*, Aug. 24, 1987). Why might this be the case?
   d. How many sermons have you heard on the subject of hell? Do we need to hear more or less about eternal punishment? Explain. How might non-Christians react to such sermons?
   e. What do you think of evangelists who go door to door, asking people if they know where they will go if they die tonight?

2. Speaking of the depression that will eventually accompany the patient's realization that he or she will die, Elisabeth Kübler-Ross writes,

   > When the terminally ill patient can no longer deny his illness, when he is forced to undergo more surgery or hospitalization, when he begins to have more symptoms or becomes weaker and thinner, he cannot smile it off anymore. His numbness or stoicism, his anger and rage, will soon be replaced with a sense of great loss.
   >
   > —On Death and Dying, p. 85

    a. Mr. Smit, Mrs. Smit, and Janet each exhibit signs of depression. Can you pick them out?

    b. Are you ever depressed? What does it feel like? How do you behave? What helps?

3. Discuss Janet's comments about how the church is handling the illness.

    a. How do you feel about bulletin announcements that explain the medical condition of church members, specifying what would and would not be helpful? Would you place such an announcement in the bulletin for yourself? How do you handle people who don't follow requests for privacy?

    b. How would your church do in a situation similar to that described in this chapter? Is your church set up to minister to people who have special needs of this sort? Who "quarterbacks" your church's ministry in such cases—the pastor, elders, deacons, or a pastoral-care committee? Is everyone in church clear as to whose responsibility such matters are?

4. Did any of the material about the intermediate stage or purgatory come as a surprise to you?

5. Does it bother you at all that we really know very little about the details of the intermediate state? Why or why not?

6. Have you ever encountered people who were dying and were unsure about their salvation? Imagine you are an elder or deacon visiting such a person. What would you say? Not say? How did Sister St. John handle Ralph?

7. Frederick Buechner writes,

> Dante saw written over the gates of Hell the words "Abandon all hope ye who enter here," but he must have seen wrong. If there is suffering life in Hell, there must also be hope in Hell, because where there is life, there is the Lord and giver of life, and where there is suffering he is there too because the suffering of the ones he loves is also his suffering.
>
> "He descended into Hell," the Creed says, and "If I make my bed in Sheol, thou art there," says the Psalmist (139:8). It seems there is no depth to which he will not sink. Maybe not even Old Scratch will be able to hold out against him forever"
>   —Wishful Thinking: A Theological ABC; New York: Harper & Row, 1973; p. 38

    a. Does anything in today's lesson lend some support to Buechner's musings?

b. Do you think Buechner is right?

c. If not, do you wish he was right? Why or why not?

d. Has the threat of hell ever made a difference in how you have chosen to live?

Closing

Each member of the group may pray silently for trust in the face of death and for confidence in the saving grace of Jesus. You may want to close by singing the final stanza of "When Peace Like a River" (*Psalter Hymnal* 489; *Trinity Hymnal* 691).

FIVE

THROUGH THE VALLEY

March 18, 1991
Dear Diary:

Dad is fading. He has an oxygen tube under his nose all the time, and the doctor told us he will need a respirator very soon if the antibiotics don't take hold this time. When the respirator starts, Dad won't be able to talk anymore. But he can't really talk now either. His throat is all dry, and he gets blue in the face trying to breathe out his sentences. I get blue watching him finish his life. This is not a good time.

When Dad is awake, he doesn't ask about world news anymore—not even about what's happening at home. Yesterday he said one thing, though, to Mom. He said that when he was dead, she should try to be her own person, that she shouldn't decide things on the basis of what she thought Dad would think or do. Dad said she had to be her own person and know her own mind. He was so blunt. Mom cried. Dad just fell asleep again.

March 21, 1991
Dear Diary:

Respirator's on. Hisses and clicks. Heart monitor hums and beeps. People speak in whispers. Dad is all huddled up tight under his sheets. They call it the fetal position, but it sure doesn't make me think of the womb. Dad can't talk, can't write. Today he stopped squeezing my hand after about lunch. I miss Dad already.

March 24, 1991
Dear Diary:
Dad died.
I can't forget him, forget this day, ever!
We were together in the waiting room. Lots of people were busy in Dad's room. Mom asked the doctor how Dad was doing. Doctor said not very good. Mom said, "No heroic measures, right?" The doctor nodded and let us in to see Dad.
We stood around the bed. Mom and John and Sally and Peter. John prayed, "Please, Lord, come quickly . . . at least for Dad, Lord, come quickly for him." The minister was there. He put his arms around us and prayed—I don't remember what. Then Dad died.
An alarm went off on the monitor, and the nurse came, and a doctor, and an orderly. We were pushed to the edge of a crowd around his bed—and then asked to leave. They let us back in a little while later, and Dad was lying straight again, his face white, room empty, machines quiet. Dead.
It was dark outside when we left. So many cars on the street, so much noise, the whole world so busy, flowing round me, leaving me behind.

◆ ◆ ◆

The dark, gloomy gray of an early spring rain invaded and pervaded Mr. Hull's senior religion classroom. It suited the class's mood. Everyone had just been told that Mr. Smit, Janet's father, had died. The "Amen" of Mr. Hull's prayer for Janet and her family was followed by an awkward silence. How do you carry on after death? The class spent a bit of time talking about the funeral's likely date and about how Janet was doing.

Mr. Hull thought back to the day of his own father's death. Even now, years later, he could feel the hot press of tears against his eyes in a flash. It wasn't unfinished business that made him sad. It wasn't that he couldn't accept his father's death. It was just that he still missed his dad. Finally, hesitantly, Mr. Hull spoke. "Well, we should get on with today's lesson. It's on the last judgment. That's something for us to think about, because as Mr. Smit's death has reminded us, we will all die. I want to make four points this morning, and I'll list them on the board as we get to them. But first, let's recap the lesson from our last class. Who will tell me the date for the last judgment? Eric?"

"No date, sir. The last judgment will happen whenever Jesus finally comes back to earth again, at the end of this age."

"Very good, Eric. But when will it be the end of this age? Julie?"

"We're not sure, though we can say a few things." Julie looked at her notes. "The Bible says things like this. 'No one knows about that day or hour, not even the angels in heaven, nor the Son, but only the Father' (Mark 13:32). And 'the Son of Man will come at an hour when you do not expect him' (Luke 12:40). Paul says that 'the day of the Lord will come like a thief in the night' (1 Thess. 5:2)."

"Right," said Mr. Hull. "We don't know when Jesus is coming back, except in the most general way. He will come back when his people have done the work he assigned to them. He will come back when the gospel has been proclaimed all around the world. And he will come back unexpectedly. Maybe tonight. Maybe on Easter. Maybe in a thousand years. But he is coming back! And among the many things that will happen then will be a universal . . . anyone know?"

"Judgment!" someone yelled out. After all, the word was printed in big letters across the chalkboard, along with the following text: "We must all appear before the judgment seat of Christ, that each one may receive what is due him for the things done while in the body, whether good or bad" (2 Cor. 5:10).

"Four points," said Mr. Hull. "First, 'We must all appear before the judgment seat.' In Hebrews 10:30, it says, 'The Lord will judge his people.' Or again, in the parable of the sheep and the goats in Matthew 25, all of them, the good and the bad, have to appear before God's judgment throne."

Julie raised her hand and asked—a bit embarrassed—"Does that mean someone like Mr. Smit has to be judged by God too? If Mr. Smit is 'with the Lord' like the thief on the cross, say, what would be the use of his being judged by Jesus when he comes again?" Julie was thinking fast now. "Do you mean that Elijah and Moses have to be judged too, even though they were with Jesus on the Mount of Transfiguration? Or that Enoch has to be judged, even though he walked and talked with God? Why?"

This was the question Mr. Hull had been waiting for. It was a good question. The class was paying close attention. Mr. Hull said, "Listen, in jokes, when someone dies and goes up to what are called the pearly gates, who does the dead person meet there?"

"Peter?" several students answered.

"Right. And what is Peter supposed to do?"

Someone said, "He's supposed to add up all the person's pluses and minuses to see whether or not this person is good enough to get into heaven."

"And does that common bit of folklore seem right?" asked Mr. Hull.

"No," said Eric. "Because, for one thing, only God can judge. And for another thing, we're saved by grace, not because our pluses outweigh our minuses."

"Right. Those are all good points, especially the one about being saved by grace, not by our works. But is there anything else wrong with jokes about Peter at the pearly gates? Kristin? Think about our class last week."

"Ah . . . judgment happens when Jesus comes back, not when we die."

"Right again," said Mr. Hull. "Neither Moses nor Mr. Smit is going to be judged until after they have been in heaven for a while, enjoying 'being with the Lord.' In fact, God in his grace already predestined all of us, his church, to be saved even before we were born. As Paul says, 'God chose us in [Christ] before the creation of the world'" (Eph. 1:4).

Mr. Hull continued. "But this raises a question. If we are saved now, why does there still need to be a last judgment?" Look carefully at the text on the board. Tell me—is there anything in the jokes about Peter at the pearly gates that does ring true?"

Karen answered, "It says in the text you wrote on the board that we will be judged with respect to 'the things done while in the body, whether good or bad.' So it looks like we are judged by our works, even if our works don't determine whether or not we're saved?" Karen finished her statement as if it were a question. This was complicated.

"Right. Point number two. Get it down. 'We are judged with respect to our works, good or bad, while we lived in the body.' Can you think of any other passages we have covered that suggest this?"

Michael-John raised his hand. "In the parable of the sheep and the goats, Jesus judges on the basis of whether or not the animals fed the hungry, gave them drink, and welcomed strangers. Those are good works."

"Anyone else? How about—get this down—Matthew 12:36, where Jesus says, 'I tell you that the men will have to give account on the day of judgment for every careless word they have spoken.' Even our thoughts will be judged, as is clear from 1 Corinthians 4:5: 'He will bring to light what is hidden in darkness and will expose the motives of men's hearts.'"

"But," said Henry, "you still haven't told us what the point of the last judgment is. What would be the use of judging Mr. Smit if he's already in heaven?"

"Anyone want to try to answer that?" asked Mr. Hull. No one did. The class was interested, but the material was pretty abstract. Mr. Hull had to move on. "Our text says that 'Each one [must] receive what is due him'—or her. Write that down as point number three. In the Greek the words could be translated something like, 'We will be judged, in order that each person may receive things in proportion to the things done in the body, either good or worthless.' The Bible is hinting that there will be degrees of reward or punishment in eternity. In other words, even though Dante's *Inferno* is mostly fabrication, there is a kernel of plausibility in his notion of different levels of reward and punishment after death.

"Take the parable of the ten minas, in Luke 19. According to this parable, a nobleman went into a far country to become the king there. Before he left, he gave each of his ten servants one mina— about three months' wages. These servants were supposed to invest their minas to earn their boss a profit. When he returned from his coronation, this nobleman found that the first servant had earned ten minas more. The nobleman rewarded this good work by giving that servant ten cities to rule over. The next servant didn't do quite as well, but he still managed to earn five more minas. This servant was given five cities to rule over—not as many as the first servant, but still quite a few. The third servant, who hid his mina and earned no profit, was given nothing—in fact, he lost even the mina he had.

"The main point of the parable is that we have to be faithful in our use of God's gifts to us. But there is another significant detail that ought not be ignored. The reward each servant received from the master turns out to be proportionate to the size profit that servant made. In a similar vein—get this passage in your notebooks— Jesus said, 'Anyone who breaks one of the least of these commandments and teaches others to do the same will be called least in the kingdom of heaven, but whoever practices and teaches these commands will be called great in the kingdom of heaven' (Matt. 5:19).

"We looked at 1 Corinthians 3:10-15 in connection with our discussion of purgatory. Remember how in this passage Paul says we have to build our Christian lives on the foundation of Jesus? But Paul also knows that once this basic allegiance is decided, some Christians will use gold and silver to build on the foundation of Jesus, while other Christians will be stingy and use only wood and straw. Then, on the day of judgment, says Paul, fire will test each person's work, and the quality each one of us has put into our Christian life will be made plain.

"Paul finishes by saying, 'If what he has built survives, he will receive his reward. If it is burned up, he will suffer loss; he himself will be saved, but only as one escaping through the flames.' Paul doesn't go into detail here, and the small number of passages in which the topic of rewards or punishment is discussed ought to make us very cautious—but it does seem as if the day of judgment will be tougher for some Christians than others. Some Christians will 'get burned' on the day of judgment, whatever that means.

Works can't make us right with Jesus, but in some mysterious way, our works still make a difference on the day of judgment. Any questions? Eric?"

"What about all those people in the world who never heard about Jesus? How will they be judged?"

"Good question. That brings up point number four. 'All persons will be judged in accordance with the light each one had.' Got that in your notebooks? Anyone have any idea what that means?"

"Does it mean that as far as God is concerned, ignorance of his law might be an excuse for breaking that law?"

"Right," said Mr. Hull, "it means something like that. Take Luke 12:47-48, where Jesus says that the 'servant who knows his master's will and does not get ready or does not do what his master wants will be beaten with many blows. But the one who does not know and does things deserving punishment will be beaten with few blows. From everyone who has been given much, much will be demanded . . . .'

"In a similar way, Jesus warns in Matthew that it will be worse for some cities on judgment day than for other cities; some cities should have known better because they had a fuller picture of God's revelation. Jesus said, 'Woe to you, Korazin! Woe to you, Bethsaida! [two Jewish cities] If the miracles that were performed in you had been performed in Tyre and Sidon [two Gentile cities], they would have repented long ago in sackcloth and ashes. But I tell you, it will be more bearable for Tyre and Sidon on the day of judgment than for you' (Matt. 11:20-22). Korazin, Bethsaida, Tyre, and Sidon are all going to be judged, you see, by the light each of them had. These passages both suggest that there will be degrees of reward and punishment after the day of judgment, and they imply that before 'passing sentence,' God will take into account whether or not the people in the dock knew his law.

"One more passage, and then we'll call it quits for the day. There's a sense in which everyone—whether they have the Bible or not—knows something of God and his law. Paul says in the book of Romans, chapter one, 'Since the creation of the world God's invisible qualities—his eternal power and divine nature—have been clearly seen, being understood from what has been made, so that men are without excuse' (v. 20). Because the heavens declare the glory of God, or because their consciences testify to God's working the law in their hearts, even people who have never read the Bible ought to know something of God.

"But, still, Paul does not assume that people without the written word of God should know the law of God in the same way as those who have the written law, like we do. In the next chapter, Paul says,

'All who sin apart from the law will also perish apart from the law, and all who sin under the law will be judged by the law' (2:12).

"That's a lot of stuff for one day, and just so that you can all get it in your notes, I'm handing out this outline, with all the texts added. Any comments? Questions? John?"

"Well, Mr. Hull, are you saying that even though we're all saved, by grace, some of us might suffer some kind of penalty because we were not all we could have been? Like, maybe some of us Christians will not have as good a time as others in heaven or on the new earth, or have a tougher judgment day than others?"

"You've got it. What, exactly, the difference, or the 'purifying fire' of 1 Corinthians 3 refers to, we can't say. How it will be better for Tyre and Sidon than for Korazin, we can't say. What being least in the kingdom of heaven looks like compared to being the greatest, we can't say. God just doesn't go into much detail here. But in some way, after the last judgment, it will be obvious that there are degrees of bliss on the earth and degrees of punishment for the lost. Yes, Kristin?"

"Well, that's kind of scary. I don't want to get personal, but there are some things I've done that were not exactly excellent, if you get my meaning. It kind of makes me afraid of the last judgment."

The class erupted with a bit of self-conscious laughter, and some other students nodded their heads in agreement.

"Sure, but don't forget," said Eric, "that like Mr. Hull says, on the judgment day, what will surprise us isn't the anger of God, but his mercy. And we all need that mercy. We're all in the same boat as you are, one way or another."

"Right, Eric," said Mr. Hull. "Who remembers why we do good works, at least according to the Heidelberg Catechism?"

"Gratitude for salvation," several answered.

"Right. But even if gratitude for salvation in Jesus Christ is the main reason for doing good works, does it mean there can be no others? Kristin, take your job at McDonald's, for example. Why do you do a good job?"

"To keep it, I guess. And because I don't want the people I work with to think I'm sponging off of them. And . . . because I want a promotion."

"Right," said Mr. Hull. "Gratitude is the first reason for doing good works. But there can be other motivations for doing good works. Wanting to be obedient to the Master of the Universe—just because he is the master, and we are servants—is a good reason for doing good works. Or, we might do good works just because we run with a crowd—the church—that does good works. And, I suppose concern about how our judgment day will go can be a reason for doing good works too!"

"Like if I'm going to be evaluated," said Kristin, "on how I'm doing my job at McDonald's, I get nervous. The evaluations always go okay, and it helps that I have a good boss and that everyone else has to go through evaluations too. But, still, I get nervous about my job evaluation."

"Listen," said Mr. Hull, "the bell is going to ring any minute. I just want to finish by saying that we don't need to be afraid about what will ultimately happen to us on judgment day. The bottom line is that we are in Christ. We are his children. Sometimes his naughty children, mind you. Sometimes his rebellious children too. But we are still God's children, and when he judges us or even punishes us, it will be always be lovingly, mercifully, and compassionately. Class dismissed."

◆ ◆ ◆

March 11, 1991
Dear Lewis:

A few months ago, when you first suggested that I write a letter in which I leave instructions for my funeral, I was appalled. I felt so much better, then, and I guess I just wasn't ready to look death so straight in the face. But now there just isn't any more room for trying to look the other way, so I'm writing you this note, as requested. Please share a copy with my family when I die. I've told them most of what is in here, but it might refresh their memory.

I'm concerned that the grandchildren get the right—albeit unpleasant—message when I die. After reading the book you gave me on children and death, I would ask of you this favor. Please take a bit of time before the funeral to explain things to them. Their parents know that you will ask, and they think it is a good idea. Please let them talk about how they are feeling. Don't step on their feelings, just let them go. Specifically, would you explain to them that I am really dead, not "just asleep" or "on a long trip." I don't want God to get blamed for my dying. Talk to them a bit about how the whole world hurts like they do, on account of sin, and about how God in Jesus has been working hard to make everything better. I'd like the kids to come to the funeral. You understand.

As I write this, I feel like it must be for someone else. It seems unreal (except when I try to swallow!). But enough of that. I suppose this feeling detached is a defense mechanism of some sort. Actually, I'm not afraid of dying—that is, I'm not afraid of what is on the other side of death. Or maybe sometimes I am, but the fears and doubts don't seem to have much power to upset me, like they used to. All in all, I'm confident when I think of meeting God, and even excited (a very little bit). I've thought a lot about your answers to my questions about the last judgment, especially to your (hesitant, I'll admit) musings on degrees of bliss in heaven. To my own way of thinking (especially when I think about my considerable shortcomings), the main thing to remember about the last judgment is that we are always talking about bliss afterward. If, when I get to the banquet table with Jesus, I find that I'm at the very far end, I will still be at banquet with Jesus. I'll never (ever!) complain because someone else is closer!

I am afraid of what has to happen before I die. I know there will be a respirator. If I could do without, I would. But there is always that chance that the pneumonia will be brought under control. Still I'm afraid of the respirator, and the tubes, and the long nights, and the inability to talk, and I guess I'm afraid of having even more pain than I have now. If there is any way to avoid it, please don't let them use all that intensive-care-unit high-tech stuff to keep me alive an extra week or two. It's bad enough to die. I don't want to be crucified on top of it.

I still have not even gotten to the main point of this letter, the funeral. The family knows what I want, basically, but let me just review it (again, I can hardly believe I'm doing this. It feels . . . well . . . ghostly).

Please, a simple, plain, cloth-covered casket. I'd like the visitation to be in the church, because that is our church family's house. The funeral home seems so antiseptic. Please, only one evening of visitation. The coffin should be closed. There is no way my shrunken body will give anyone (as Calvin thought a funeral should) a visible reminder of our hope in the resurrection. A picture on the coffin would be better. However, please make sure that the grandkids and the family and my very closest friends (Diane knows who) get a chance before or after the visitation to see the body, for "closure's sake" as you put it.

I'd like there to be a private burial service for the family and closest friends before the memorial service. That way, at the memorial service, you can emphasize that the last word is not the dead body, but our hope for the resurrection. At least that's how I see it, and I hope you can work with that. I know it's going to be busy for you, so I won't burden you by asking you to preach on a specific text. But please read Psalm 104, or a portion of it—especially the words about how God provides wine and oil to make our faces shine.

As for the order of service, do whatever you think best. I would like to have "Seek Ye First the Kingdom of God" sung at the funeral, with the descant. And I'd like the congregation to sing "Praise the Lord with the Sound of Trumpets" on the next Sunday, as my last hymn-sing request.

Lewis, you are a good friend. You listen when I have nothing to say, and you answer questions I hardly dare ask. Thank you, and shalom, till we meet again, in Jerusalem.

Ralph Smit

Suggestions for Group Session

Opening

Read two Scripture passages that offer comfort to the dying and the bereaved: Romans 8:18-39 and Psalm 23.

For Discussion

1. Have you or has anyone in your group had to live through a time when the life of a loved one was artificially extended through the use of high-tech medicine? Share the circumstances with the class. How did you feel? Do you wish you could have done anything differently? How were the choices presented to you? Was a pastor involved? Were you (are you) personally ready to deal with such eventualities in a biblically informed way?

2. Take a look at the "Living Will" printed on the facing page. Is it a good idea to have such a document? Would you ever suggest such a document to someone else or have one written up for yourself? What is the legal status of such an instrument in your state or province?

3. How do you feel about the Smit family decision not to use "extraordinary means" to keep Mr. Smit alive?

4. Mr. Hull made four basic points in his presentation on the last judgment. Divide into four groups, each group focusing on and summarizing one point. Each group should also ask itself if anyone present is surprised by that point. Do they find it comforting? Why or why not?

5. We are saved by grace but judged for our works. How do you feel about the prospect of being judged by Jesus when he returns?

6. Mr. Smit is never happy about his illness or impending death. But he seems, toward the end, to come to accept it. How is this evident in this chapter?

Disclaimer: Remember that this document is an expression of your wishes only. You have no guarantee that it will be binding upon your physician, relatives, or the hospital in which you are being cared for.

"Living Will"

TO MY FAMILY, MY PHYSICIAN,
MY LAWYER, MY CLERGYMAN

TO ANY MEDICAL FACILITY IN WHOSE CARE
I HAPPEN TO BE

TO ANY INDIVIDUAL WHO MAY BECOME RESPONSIBLE
FOR MY HEALTH, WELFARE, OR AFFAIRS

Death is as much a reality as birth, growth, maturity and old age. It is the one certainty of life. If the time comes when I, _____ can no longer take part in decisions for my own future, let this statement stand as an expression of my wishes, while I am still of sound mind.

If the situation should arise in which there is no reasonable expectation of my recovery from physical or mental disability, then I request that medication be mercifully administered to me to alleviate suffering, and that I be allowed to die and not be kept alive by artificial means or "heroic measures." I do not fear death itself as much as the indignities of deterioration, dependence and hopeless pain.

This request is made after careful consideration. I hope you who care for me will feel morally bound to follow its mandate. I recognize that this appears to place heavy responsibility upon you, but it is with the intention of relieving you of such responsibility and of placing it upon myself in accordance with my strong convictions, that this statement is made.

In accordance with the above paragraph, I hereby direct that any costs arising out of any legal action taken against one or more of the above-mentioned parties shall be borne by my estate and further direct should any judgment be rendered against one or more of the said parties that such party(ies) be indemnified and saved harmless out of the proceeds of my estate.

_____
(Signed)

_____
(Date)

_____
(Witness)

_____
(Witness)

Copies of this request have been given to _____

_____

7. Not all people are as well prepared to die as Mr. Smit. How would you feel about Mr. Smit if he had died directly after the failed miracle attempt?
8. Is Mr. Smit's last letter morbid or appropriate? Will you write such a letter and leave it with your spouse or friend? Why?
9. Take some time to plan out how you would like your funeral to go. Say something about each of the following items:
   - Coffin choice. Do you wish to have an open or a closed coffin? If you think an open coffin is appropriate? When and where?
   - Visiting hours. Where, how often?
   - Minister's involvement. When and where do you hope the minister will be with your family? Are your expectations realistic? Will you remunerate the pastor? Is the minister clear about such expectations, or does he or she have to guess?
   - Memorial and graveside services. Are there songs you would like to sing? Scripture passages you would like read? Are there special people you would like to have sing?
   - Young children. Should they come?
10. How would you answer the following questions, asked by one of Mr. Smit's grandchildren?
    - Where is Grandpa?
    - Why did God let Grandpa die?
    - Will I ever see Grandpa again?
    - Why does Grandpa have all those wires around him (in the hospital)?
    - Can I touch Grandpa (in the coffin)?
    - I want to say something to Grandpa (in the coffin). May I?
    - Does Grandpa want to be in heaven instead of with us?
11. John Calvin believed that the careful preparation of bodies for burial and the actual burial of the bodies themselves are visible ways by which Christians can underline their faith in bodily resurrection. Calvin asks, for example, "Why should a burial rite arise . . . unless to let men know that a new life was prepared for the bodies laid away?" But Calvin also says, "Since God has all the elements ready at his bidding, no difficulty will hinder his commanding earth, waters, and fire to restore what they seem to have consumed" (*Institutes,* 3,xxv,8, pp. 1002-3). What do you think? Is burial, as opposed to cremation, required by Scripture?

Closing
Offer sentence prayers, each of you praying for comfort and strength for a person or family you know who is grieving over the death of someone they loved. You may wish to close by quietly singing the twenty-third Psalm (*Psalter Hymnal* 23, 161, 162, or 550; *Rejoice in the Lord* 89 or 90).

SIX

VICTORY!

March 30, 1991
Dear Diary,
    It's been almost a week already. All the "older" relatives went home yesterday, and now just Peter, John and Sally, and the kids are here. It's almost quiet in the house. Actually, after the busyness of the funeral, it's nice to just float around the house quietly. No one is rushing off to go shopping or to the coffee shop—like we usually do when we're all together. The quiet at home is how I want to feel inside.
    In church we've often sung "My Jesus, I Love Thee": "In mansions of glory and endless delight / I'll ever adore thee in heaven so bright"; and "Amazing Grace": "When we've been there ten thousand years, / bright shining as the sun, / we've no less days to sing God's praise / than when we'd first begun." Those songs had better have it wrong. Spending forever in that kind of heaven—white-robed, singing songs, and maybe plucking harps, the way those songs suggest—doesn't sound appealing to me. Dad would hate it.
    Tomorrow is Easter. Mom wants us to go to the sunrise service—in the cemetery. It looked awful on the day after the funeral. Snow everywhere, except by the grave, where they laid a carpet of fake green grass under a carnival tent—as if it were a picnic.
    I wonder what it will be like to go back.

❖ ❖ ❖

Mark Hull sat in his office at home and watched Mr. Friedrich Konig trudge through the snow and slush up to his front door. As Mark waited, he was vaguely aware of feeling knots in his stomach. Two days ago, in class, he had suggested that when Jesus returned, this old earth would not be destroyed but rather cleansed and made new. Some students, the ones who had been listening, had duly reported this fact at home. Three parents had called him that night to object to this teaching. Mr. Konig had called, too, and had made it plain that he was seriously thinking of taking his children out of the school and transferring them to the Christian Academy, where they would be taught the "inerrant Bible and its literal interpretation." Mark had asked Mr. Konig over to discuss the matter.

Happy Valley Christian High could ill afford to lose more supporting families. Things were tight already. The latest round of defections had begun when a drama class attended a play that some parents found objectionable on account of the profanity. Next the creation/evolution issue washed over the school, and more supporting families withdrew when the board affirmed one teacher in her teaching of theistic evolution as a defendable Christian approach to beginnings.

Mark got up to meet Mr. Konig at the door and to show him into his office. After Mark brought out some coffee and donuts, Mr. Konig got straight to the point. "Mark, you made a big mistake in class the other day. You contradicted the plain teaching of Scripture when you said this world will not be destroyed when Jesus comes again. Your notion that this world can be made new sounds 'New Ageish' to me—seeing how you glorify nature and all that. It's just another example of what I see happening over and over in the school. You don't interpret Scripture plainly or literally. You treat Scripture like a dancing bear, making it do all sorts of tricks that are unnatural and wrong. I know you mean well, Mark, but why should I pay so much money for Christian education if my children are being misled? I would rather send them to the public school, where at least the devil doesn't walk the hallways in padded slippers. Or to the Christian Academy."

"Well, Mr. Konig . . ."

"Come on, Mark. We're both adults. Just because I lend all you teachers mortgage money even though you really don't qualify doesn't mean we can't talk man to man. Call me Fred."

"Okay . . . ah . . . Fred." Mark was a bit embarrassed, though he wasn't sure if it was for himself or "Fred." He went on. "Why do you think, exactly, that this earth is going to be totally destroyed? What Scripture do you think supports your view?"

"I studied up, Mark, before I came here. I know of three texts that literally teach the destruction of this earth. First, there is Revelation 21:1, where it says, 'Then I saw a new heaven and a new earth, for the first heaven and the first earth had passed away, and there was no longer any sea.' The important words are 'passed away.' If you would read that literally, it means that they will be gone, no more, destroyed!"

"The other texts, Fred?"

"Only need one, since Scripture can't contradict Scripture, you know. But I have two other texts anyway. In Matthew 24:29 Jesus says, 'The sun will be darkened, and the moon will not give its light; the stars will fall from the sky, and the heavenly bodies will be shaken.' It sounds to me like this planet will be blasted out of orbit, if you read that plainly. Then there is 2 Peter 3:10-12, which says, 'The elements will be destroyed by fire and the earth and everything in it will be laid bare . . . . That day will bring about the destruction of the heavens by fire, and the elements will melt in the heat.' Now, no earth will survive such a destruction and fire! Here, I've written the texts out for you, so we can discuss them."

Mark looked over the texts that Mr. Konig gave him and reread them for himself. He knew these texts, of course. To his way of thinking, these passages made it clear, at the very least, that cataclysmic events would accompany Jesus' return to this earth—events that would add up to a divine judgment against the world's sin. He said so to Mr. Konig.

"Sure, of course you are right. But these texts say more. They say that the earth will be destroyed! You must not take anything away from Scripture. Not a jot or a tittle, Mark. Once you open the door to changing what Scripture says to suit yourself, the world will come pouring in and drown your faith. It must not be done."

Mr. Konig was unthinkingly equating his personal interpretation of the text with what he figured the text literally said, thought Mark. He told Fred so, and then went on to point out that 2 Peter 3:6 actually likened the fire of judgment to the waters of Noah's flood, suggesting that the fire doesn't annihilate the world so much as cleanse it of the effects of sin—much the same way as the flood did—without utterly destroying the world. Mark explained to Mr. Konig that the Matthew passage did not actually say that this earth would be destroyed, though it would be easy to read that into the passage if you were already convinced.

"You are wrong, Mr. Hull, I'm sad to say. Just because the destruction of the elements is compared to the destruction of the earth under Noah does not mean they are the same kind of destruction. For one thing, fire destroys much more completely than water. And I still have the Revelation passage which says that there will be a new heaven and earth—that means the first heaven and earth do have to be destroyed."

Mark handed a piece of paper to Mr. Konig. "Before you came, I pulled some stuff together based on one of the better books about the endtimes, by Professor Hoekema. He lists four reasons why we should think of the new earth as a renewed present earth. You've probably got the book too, but let's go through the four reasons just to make sure we understand them well."

"Sure, but wasn't he one of the professors at the seminary where they teach about evolution and women in office? The seminary isn't what it used to be, you know."

"Maybe not, Fred. But this professor taught there many years ago. Anyway, let's look at what he has to say and judge it by looking at Scripture ourselves. Fair enough?" Mark had to smile, almost in spite of himself. Fred Konig wouldn't be put into a corner, and he was very combative. But Fred was obviously enjoying this debate with a teacher, too, and savoring it apart from any intent to get at the school or himself. That was okay.

"Well, look, Fred. We ought to start with what the texts say in the Greek. First, there are two Greek words for 'new.' One of them is *neos* —from which we derive our English word new. *Neos* means that 'something is new in time—that it never before existed.' But the Greek word used in the phrase 'a new heaven and a new earth' in Revelation and in 2 Peter 3:13 is *Kainos*, and it means 'new in nature or quality.' One could even argue for the translation 'a reconditioned earth and heaven.'"

"Ah, yes, but it isn't really fair to go to the Greek, Mark, because Scripture is supposed to be clear, perspicuous, to the everyday reader—so we confess, don't we? How can that be true if every time we want to decide something, learned people pull out the Greek to show up us common people in the pew?"

"Fred, how can you say that? Our tradition has always honored good scholarship. You can check out what I'm saying in any good Bible dictionary or commentary. But about this clarity, or perspicuity: we believe that Scripture is clear about salvation, but not necessarily about everything else. Some things about the Bible and some doctrines are hard to understand. For example, even though both you and your Baptist friends over at the academy agree that Scripture ought to be read literally, you still disagree about baptism and about the timetable for Jesus' second coming. Agreeing that you will both take Scripture literally doesn't mean you won't have conflicts of interpretation. You and I and the Baptists all take Scripture seriously as God's infallible Word. But being fallible humans, we can still differ on its interpretation."

"Well, I'm not convinced. New is new. You are confusing the reading of Scripture, which anyone can do, with theology. That is dangerous!"

"Well, let me read some Scripture for you then." Mark was feeling frustrated, feeling as if Fred wasn't willing to be engaged. "How about some Scripture that clearly says this old earth will not be destroyed? In Romans 8:20-21 Paul writes that 'the creation itself will be liberated from its bondage to decay and brought into the glorious freedom of the children of God.' What Paul means is that this world is longing for liberation because it knows a new day is coming when it will be freed from the effects of human sin."

"Ah, yes, but, Mark, that is obviously a figure of speech, don't you think? Creation cannot 'long' for liberation, because creation is not alive. That would be a New Age notion. So Paul is using a figure of speech to make it plain how much we ought to desire the new heaven and earth."

"Fred," Mark said with just a trace of frustration, "Paul's plain sense here is that this creation is going to be liberated—not that there will be a new creation. Either you take all of Scripture literally, like you say, including Romans 8, or, like me, you own up to the fact that interpreting Scripture isn't that simple."

"Maybe. What else do you have?"

"An analogy. Remember how when Jesus arose from the grave, his new body was similar to yet different from his first body? Jesus' resurrection body was recognizably his first body since it even bore the scars he suffered in the crucifixion. But the resurrection body was different too. Jesus could pass through doors, for example, and he was not always immediately recognized by former friends, such as Mary and the men from Emmaus. Just so, the new earth will be recognizably this earth, though it will be different too—renewed and remade, just as Jesus' resurrection body was and ours will be."

Mark could see that Fred was about to object, so he plowed quickly on to his last point. He wanted to get all his information out before Fred said more, in the hope that all of it together would help Fred reconsider.

"Listen, one more thing, Fred. If God annihilated this world, Satan would really have won a great victory. Satan would have succeeded in so ruining God's creation that God could do nothing else but throw it out like an old rag. But Satan didn't win that kind of victory; on the contrary, Satan was decisively defeated. God is going to show just how defeated Satan is by ridding this world of all the ill that Satan did to it . . . but saving the world itself."

"Well, I don't know Mark. Seems like you are using reason instead of revelation."

"Would you want me to say unreasonable things? After all, most of our Reformed doctrines are, at least in part, dependent on sound reasoning from Scripture to life."

"Yeah, well, if this world won't be annihilated, what will happen to it?"

"In Acts 3:19-26 Peter suggests that when Jesus returns, this world will be refreshed and restored. Think of an old piece of walnut furniture that has been used and abused for a lifetime. The varnish is pitted, the legs are loose, and the whole thing is green. Through time, what was once a valuable and beautiful walnut bureau becomes a rotting old chest.

"What Jesus does, when he comes again, is strip that bureau of its old paint and ruined veneer. Jesus will take the thing apart, screw by screw, sand it, repair it, and lovingly glue it back together, till it shines with its original glory. So, says Peter, when Jesus comes back, he will refresh and restore this earth. He will go as far, if necessary, as taking this whole earth apart, but it will be for the restoration of this earth, not its destruction and annihilation.

"In other words, there will be a lot of continuity between this world and the next one. The apostle John says in Revelation 14:13 that those who die before Jesus' return 'will rest from their labor, for their deeds will follow them,' presumably into life everlasting. What you do now, Fred, in this world, can have an eternal impact in the next. Say you lend money to a company that wants to install more efficient emissions scrubbers. The cleaner air that results might well be one of the good things from this earth that will be carried over in the new. Or again, in 1 Corinthians 3:10-14 Paul promises that if we build on the foundation of Jesus using gold, silver, and costly stones, what we build will survive the fire of judgment, and we will be rewarded for it."

"Mark, you must stick to the point. I'm talking about Revelation 21:1, not my job at the bank."

"But there is a connection, Fred. The new earth will not be another earth; it will be this earth—and if you will permit me to dream in Christ for a moment, my hope is that it will be this old earth's forests, fields, cities, streets, and people that are the scene of redemption. Today our world looks like a battlefield, full of rubble, brokenness, and wounded hurting people. But when Jesus returns, this battlefield will be transformed into a field of victory. As Psalm 126 promises, what we sow now with tears will one day ripen so that it can be reaped and brought home. And you can do some of that sowing, now, by your choices about what merits investment at the bank."

"Well, I'm not convinced. Bankers deal with car loans and mortgages and profits. But I'll study the matter further."

"Fred, let me share with you why I think this doctrine of a renewed earth is so wonderful! It accents redemption, the fact that people and things that are broken can be renewed in Jesus—even before he comes again. Think of how Paul says in 2 Corinthians 5:17 that 'if anyone is in Christ, he is a new creation; the old has gone, the new has come!' Shouldn't some of that newness we have already now rub off on the world and last forever and ever, even into the new earth? In fact, that's what God wants us to do in this world, as kingdom agents, until he comes again. God wants us to be busy cleaning out the garden as a promise and sign of the things to come.

"That's why your job at the bank does make a difference for eternity. You shouldn't make decisions solely on the basis of what will bring the greatest profit. After all, we can't take the money we make now with us into eternal life. What we might take with us is the environment, or beautiful literature, or perhaps even a factory that makes useful products. These are the sort of treasures we ought to be storing up for heaven on earth, the sort of treasures you can work for from your important position in the bank."

Mark noticed that Fred's eyes were glazing over. Of course, Mark had stopped talking to Fred and begun scolding him instead. Mark decided enough was enough. "You know, Fred, we have a good Christian school. We don't agree on everything, but all of us teachers are committed to searching God's Word, understanding it, and applying it to the real world out there."

"It's true that my kids love it there. It will be hard to take them out. I won't do it lightly. But as you can see, we do not have the same ideas about Scripture. I'll think about it." With that, they shook hands, and Fred left.

♦ ♦ ♦

Janet and her mother stood on the outer edge of the small group who had come out for the Easter sunrise service. The sun was just coming over the trees in the distance, and the glare made it hard for Janet to see the minister.

They had not had to walk past Dad's grave. It was just visible out of the corner of Janet's eye a hundred yards or so away. As she and her mother stood leaning against each other, as if to ward off the cold, Janet kept looking sideways at the grave, unable to keep her eyes averted.

And yet she listened too—especially when the minister mentioned her father's name. He was saying, "Ralph Smit was telling me a few weeks ago about a conversation he overheard in the patient lounge. Some aides were talking about makeup, about moisturizers and liquid base foundations, about rubbing in color versus brushing on blush. Ralph's own body was wasting away then, so the conversation naturally made Ralph think about how he wished it wasn't so, and from there, he thought about how he wished the resurrection was now. He asked me about the resurrection, about what made me so sure, anyway, that we would get new bodies.

"So I shared these words with Ralph, from 1 Corinthians 15:22-23, where it says, 'In Christ all will be made alive. But each in his own turn: Christ, the firstfruits; then, when he comes again, those who belong to him.'

"How do we know? How do we know that Ralph or any of our other brothers and sisters who are buried in this place will rise with new bodies?

"We know because we have seen it happen once already. Jesus—a human person like you and me, a person who died and was buried, just like Ralph— has risen from the grave! In rising first, Jesus demonstrated that we all can rise. Jesus' resurrection is like a travel poster of our future resurrection destination. When we look at the travel poster in Scripture, we can rest assured that the resurrection destination is real, that Jesus went there first to have the picture taken."

Janet thought about that travel poster—about Jesus appearing to Mary and to the disciples. She looked at the grave of her father, and in a deep and mysterious way she made the connection between death and life. Her eyes filled with tears. She wiped them off on her mother's shoulder, felt her mother pull her arm tighter around Janet's shoulder.

"Paul is saying that what happened to Jesus in the flesh is encouragement for us in the flesh. Imagine that we are playing a baseball game. In the bottom of the third inning, in the middle of human history, Jesus hit a grand-slam that cemented the game. Jesus' resurrection from the dead assured us of the final outcome of the game. We shall be victorious.

"One thing more, though—something that's important for us who still live with our old bodies to hear. Jesus' grand slam doesn't mean the game is over. After Jesus' resurrection, we still have to persevere to the bottom of the ninth. We have to, as Paul says in verse 58, stand firm. We have to give ourselves over to the same work Jesus was busy with—because we know that what Jesus did in the third inning was not in vain. Now is no time for us to quit and to forfeit what Christ has won.

"Some people think that giving their bodies the royal treatment involves spending hours and hours before a mirror, or getting a liposuction, or taking out a membership in a fancy health club. It's true that treating your body with respect and care is to be commended. But the best way to treat yourself royally is to accept your commission from the King, to accept your job as the king's 'ambassador of reconciliation.'

"We don't have to pine after new bodies today (though we can hope for them tomorrow), because we have something exciting to do with our lives right now. We can do what Jesus did when he walked on this planet. We can heal the sick, feed the hungry, lay down our lives, time, and talents to proclaim the good news of God's love for his human children."

The minister went on for some time, but Janet wasn't listening anymore. She thought of her dying father, sunken in his hospital bed, holding her hand when she had come to hold his, listening to her when she had come to listen. She thought of his prayers for healing and his reluctant giving up of the good gift of life. Dad was dead. She missed him much. But, for Christ's sake, she was going to move on.

Suggestions for Group Session

Opening
Read 1 Corinthians 15, a beautiful account of the resurrection of Christ, the resurrection of the dead, and the resurrection body.

For Discussion

1. Think about the moment you first heard of the death of a family member (parent, child, sibling, grandparent)—someone you felt very close to. Where were you when you heard about the death? Who was present? Who told you about the death? In what words? How did you feel?

2. In order to work through those feelings, draw a circle and divide it into pie shapes according to the kinds of feelings you had; give each feeling as much space in the circle as it had in your life. Some feelings you might have experienced are shock, sadness, fear, anger, relief, denial, depression, and embarrassment. For each feeling that applied, choose a color that fits that feeling and then color in the circle. Share your circle with the class and explain it. (Adapted from *CPJ-RPC,* March 1988, Barbara M. Sourkes.)

3. How exact can our knowledge be about what happens to us after we die? If you were asked by an unbeliever what Christians believe about the afterlife, what things would you feel confident to share with this person?

4. Martin Luther is reputed to have said once that even if he learned the Lord would return tomorrow, he would still plant the tree he had planned to plant today. Would you? Explain.

5. How does the fact of Jesus' resurrection comfort and encourage us today?

6. How will Janet cope with the future? Give evidence for your answer.

7. Do you know anyone who is not coping well with the death of someone they loved? Be careful about mentioning names, but if you know such a person, share with the class what you can do to encourage him or her.

Closing

Conclude your final session together with a celebration of the resurrection. Begin by reading a few resurrection promises from Scripture: John 11:25; Romans 6:5-7; Philippians 3:7-11; 1 Peter 1:3-9. You may also wish to sing a few resurrection hymns: "Crown Him with Many Crowns" (*Psalter Hymnal* 410; *Rejoice in the Lord* 600; *Trinity Hymnal* 295), "Christ the Lord Is Risen Today" (*Psalter Hymnal* 388; *Rejoice in the Lord* 325; *Trinity Hymnal* 277), "Praise the Savior Now and Ever" (*Psalter Hymnal* 400; *Trinity Hymnal* 243).

Conclude your session with a prayer or prayers of thanksgiving for Jesus' victory over death and promise of eternal life.

SUGGESTED READING LIST

Clouse, Robert, ed. *The Meaning of the Millennium.* Downers Grove, IL: InterVarsity Press, 1979. *A good summary of the three major views on how and when Jesus will come again. Includes a contribution by Anthony Hoekema.*

Cooper, John. *Body, Soul, and Life Everlasting.* Grand Rapids, MI: Eerdmans, 1989. *Cooper explores questions concerning what happens when we die.*

DePaola, Tomie. *Nana Upstairs & Nana Downstairs.* New York: Puffin Books, 1973. *The story of a little boy who watches his grandmother grow old and die. DePaola's books are beautifully illustrated, and the stories are well told. Parents will need to say more about what happens after death, however, than DePaola does here.*

Hoekema, Anthony. *The Bible and the Future.* Grand Rapids, MI: Eerdmans, 1979. *This is the standard Reformed treatment on the second coming of Jesus and all that precedes and follows it. Very readable.*

Kelsey, Morton. *Healing and Christianity.* New York: Harper and Row, 1973. *This book is especially valuable for its treatment of signs and wonders in the early church.*

Kop, Ruth. *Where Has Grandpa Gone?* Grand Rapids, MI: Zondervan, 1983. *A helpful guide for parents who wish to be well prepared to help their children cope with grief and loss.*

Kübler-Ross, Elisabeth, ed. *Living with Death and Dying.* New York: Macmillan Publishing Co., 1982. *Contains interesting material on dealing with terminally ill persons, including children.*

Kübler-Ross, Elisabeth. *On Death and Dying.* New York: Macmillan Publishing Co., 1969. *The book that touched off the "stages of death and dying" discussion.*

Lewis, C.S. *A Grief Observed.* New York: Harper and Row, 1961. *Perhaps Lewis's most somber book, written in the spirit of Psalm 88.*

Smedes, Lewis. *How Can It Be All Right When Everything Is All Wrong?* New York: Harper and Row, 1982.

Smedes, Lewis, ed. *Ministry and the Miraculous.* Pasadena, CA: Fuller Theological Seminary, 1987. *The heart of this book tackles the credibility of the miraculous in today's church. A must-read and a corrective to Kelsey.*

Smedes, Lewis. "Of Miracles and Suffering," *The Reformed Journal*, February 1989, pp. 14-21. *Smedes struggles with putting personal miracles front and center at a time when the whole world is crying out for redemption.*

Tolstoy, Leo. *The Death of Ivan Ilych. A must-read for everyone who is thinking about this topic. An especially poignant portrayal of the loneliness of dying.*

Vogel, Linda Jane. *Helping a Child Understand Death.* Philadelphia: Fortress Press, 1975. *An excellent book.*

Wolterstorff, Nicholas. *Lament for a Son.* Grand Rapids, MI: Eerdmans, 1987. *Wolterstorff's autobiographical account of his personal struggle with sorrow, anger, and especially with God after the death of his son. Highly recommended.*

Yancy, Philip. *Disappointment with God.* Grand Rapids, MI: Zondervan, 1988.

Yancy, Philip. *Where Is God When It Hurts?* Grand Rapids, MI: Zondervan, 1977. *A fine, pastoral book about pain and evil.*